You Are Enough
The 90-Day Self-Love Breakthrough

thedailywellness.com

You Are Enough
The 90-Day Self-Love Breakthrough

Copyright © 2025 Daily Media Group US LLC
All rights reserved.

No part of this journal may be reproduced, distributed, or transmitted in any form or by any means, including photocopying, recording, or other electronic or mechanical methods, without the prior written permission of the publisher, except in the case of brief quotations embodied in critical reviews and certain other noncommercial uses permitted by copyright law.

First Edition: 2025
ISBN: 979-8-9938294-0-1

Published by:
Daily Media Group US LLC

For inquiries, permissions, or bulk orders:
support@thedailywellness.com

Proudly printed and manufactured in the USA

The 90-Day Self-Love Breakthrough

A guided journey from self-criticism to self-compassion

Name: _____

Date Started: _____

"The relationship you have with yourself sets the foundation for everything else in your life."

Dear Reader,

Welcome to a journey that could change everything—not by changing who you are, but by changing how you see and treat yourself.

If you're holding this journal, you've already taken the most important step: choosing yourself. Perhaps you're tired of the critical inner voice that never seems satisfied. Maybe you've realized that no amount of external achievement quiets the feeling of not being enough. Or possibly, you're simply ready to experience what life feels like when lived from a place of self-love rather than self-doubt.

Whatever brought you here, you belong here.

About This Journey

This isn't another self-help program promising overnight transformation. This is a gentle, structured path based on psychological research and thousands of hours of clinical practice.

Over 90 days, you'll build five foundational practices:
1. Transforming self-criticism into self-awareness
2. Ending self-neglect through intentional self-care
3. Developing genuine self-acceptance
4. Cultivating deep self-compassion
5. Establishing sustainable self-love

A Personal Note

I've walked this path myself, from a place of harsh self-judgment to one of genuine self-compassion. This journal contains what I wish I'd known years ago: that self-love isn't selfish, it's essential. That you can't hate yourself into becoming someone you love. And that the person you're trying to become—you already are.

Your journey starts now. Be patient with yourself. Trust the process. You're exactly where you need to be.

With compassion and hope,
The Daily Wellness Team

Get Your FREE Self-Love Toolkit!

Transform Your 90-Day Journey with $47 Worth of Digital Gifts – Absolutely FREE!

We believe you deserve every tool for success. That's why we've created exclusive FREE resources to support your self-love breakthrough – no catch, no credit card, just instant access to everything you need.

What's Included in Your Free Toolkit:

- ✓ 30-Day Self-Love Guided Meditations (audio)
- ✓ Daily Progress & Mood Trackers (printable)
- ✓ Self-Love Affirmation Library (50+ affirmations)
- ✓ Emergency Self-Love Rescue Kit (for tough days)
- ✓ Transformational Worksheets & PDFs
- ✓ Bonus Surprises Worth $97+

Claim Your FREE Gifts Now!

Scan with your phone camera

Or visit: http://store.thedailywellness.com/freeselflovegifts

3 Simple Steps:
1. Scan the QR code above
2. Enter your email
3. Get instant access to everything for FREE!

Questions? Email: support@thedailywellness.com

Don't wait – claim your free resources now and give yourself every tool for success.

Table of Contents

Your 90-Day Journey

PHASE 1: FOUNDATION (Days 1-30)
Building Your Core Practices

Introduction & Assessment 5

Section 1: Self-Criticism 14
Days 1-6: Transforming your inner dialogue

Section 2: Self-Neglect 22
Days 7-12: Reclaiming your worth through self-care

Section 3: Self-Acceptance 32
Days 13-18: Embracing your whole self

Section 4: Self-Compassion 41
Days 19-24: Treating yourself with kindness

Section 5: Self-Love 49
Days 25-30: The foundation of your worth

Transition: From Learning to Living 59

PHASE 2: PRACTICE (Days 31-90)
Your 60-Day Integration Journey

Month 1: Building Awareness 64
Weeks 1-4 of daily practice (Days 31-58)

Month 2: Deepening Practice 126
Weeks 5-8 of daily practice (Days 59-86)

PHASE 3: INTEGRATION (Days 87-90)
Your Final Integration 168
Sustaining your transformation

Your Transformation Journey

This is not about becoming a different person.

It's about finally becoming who you've always been beneath the criticism, neglect, and self-doubt.

The Three Phases

PHASE 1: FOUNDATION

You'll spend 30 days building your foundation through five core sections. Each section includes:
- Understanding the concept
- Identifying your patterns
- Practical exercises
- Daily practices
- Progress tracking

PHASE 2: PRACTICE

Your 60-day practice journal where knowledge becomes embodied wisdom through:
- Daily morning intentions
- Evening reflections
- Weekly themes
- Progress tracking
- Flexible practice options

PHASE 3: INTEGRATION

Your final days to consolidate gains, celebrate growth, and create your sustainable practice.

What You'll Experience

- **Weeks 1-2:** Awareness and recognition of patterns
- **Weeks 3-4:** Resistance and breakthrough moments
- **Weeks 5-8:** New habits forming, old patterns softening
- **Weeks 9-12:** Integration and authentic self-expression
- **Week 13:** Celebration and sustainable practice design

Realistic Expectations

- **Progress won't be linear**—expect ups and downs
- **Some days will feel harder** than others
- **Resistance is normal** and part of the process
- Small shifts create **profound changes over time**
- **You're rewiring years of conditioning**—be patient

The Journey from Criticism to Confidence

The Transformation Process
Current State → Transitional Phase → Transformed State

Harsh critic → Noticing the voice → Compassionate observer
Self-neglect → Setting boundaries → Consistent self-care
Rejection → Tolerating yourself → Genuine acceptance
Self-attack → Neutral observation → Self-compassion
Worthlessness → Questioning worth → Inherent value

Your Growth Edge

Growth happens at the edge of your comfort zone.
This journey will gently stretch you:

Comfort Zone:
Where you are now

Growth Zone:
Where transformation happens

Panic Zone:
Too much, too fast

We'll keep you in the growth zone—challenged but not overwhelmed.

Where Are You Starting?

Rate each statement from 1 (never) to 10 (always).

Self-Criticism
I notice my critical thoughts without believing them: _____
I speak to myself with kindness: _____
I can interrupt negative self-talk: _____

Self-Care
I prioritize my physical needs: _____
I honor my emotional needs: _____
I take breaks without guilt: _____

Self-Acceptance
I accept my imperfections: _____
I embrace all parts of myself: _____
I am comfortable being myself: _____

Self-Compassion
I comfort myself when struggling: _____
I treat myself as a good friend: _____
I forgive my mistakes easily: _____

Self-Love
I believe I deserve good things: _____
I celebrate my uniqueness: _____
I know my inherent worth: _____

Total Score: _____ / 150

> **Score Ranges:**
> - 30-60: Strong foundation needed (perfect place to start)
> - 61-90: Some practices in place (ready to deepen)
> - 91-120: Good awareness (time for consistency)
> - 121-150: Strong practice (ready for mastery)

Remember: Wherever you're starting is the perfect place. Lower scores mean more room for beautiful growth.

Your Current Relationship with Yourself

How would you describe your inner voice?
- ☐ Harsh critic
- ☐ Neutral observer
- ☐ Supportive friend
- ☐ Varies greatly
- ☐ Don't notice it

Your biggest challenge:
- ☐ Constant self-criticism
- ☐ Neglecting my needs
- ☐ Not accepting myself
- ☐ Lack of self-compassion
- ☐ Not knowing my worth

What brought you to this journal?
_____
_____
_____

Your Patterns Inventory

Check all that apply:

Thought Patterns:
- ☐ Perfectionism
- ☐ Comparison
- ☐ All-or-nothing thinking
- ☐ Mind reading
- ☐ Catastrophizing

Behavioral Patterns:
- ☐ People-pleasing
- ☐ Overworking
- ☐ Procrastination
- ☐ Isolation
- ☐ Self-sabotage

Emotional Patterns:
- ☐ Shame spirals
- ☐ Anxiety loops
- ☐ Numbness
- ☐ Overwhelm
- ☐ Resentment

Your Strengths Foundation

Even in struggle, you have strengths. Check yours:
- ☐ Resilience (you're still here)
- ☐ Hope (you're trying)
- ☐ Courage (you're starting)
- ☐ Awareness (you recognize patterns)
- ☐ Commitment (you got this journal)

Three qualities I appreciate about myself:
1. _____
2. _____
3. _____

You Don't Have to Do This Alone

Your Inner Circle
- Person I trust most: _____
- How they can support me: _____
- Someone who believes in me: _____
- How I'll include them: _____

Professional Support (if applicable)
- Therapist/Counselor: _____
- Coach/Mentor: _____
- Healthcare provider: _____

Community Support
- Online community: _____
- Local support group: _____
- Workout buddy: _____
- Accountability partner: _____

Boundaries for Your Journey

I need to protect my practice from:
- Negative people: _____
- Time drains: _____
- Energy vampires: _____
- Old habits: _____

I will create safety by:
- Setting phone boundaries
- Scheduling practice time
- Saying no to: _____
- Asking for: _____

Emergency Support Plan

When I'm struggling, I will:
1. First: _____
2. Then: _____
3. Call: _____
4. Remember: _____

Crisis Resources:
- National Crisis Line: 988
- Crisis Text Line: Text HOME to 741741
- Your local resource: _____

Why This Journey Matters to You

Complete these prompts thoughtfully.

I am ready to transform my relationship with myself because:
_____
_____

What I most want to change:
_____
_____

What I hope to feel in 90 days:
_____
_____

Who I'm doing this for (hint: yourself first):
_____
_____

Your 90-Day Vision

Imagine yourself 90 days from now...

How you speak to yourself:
_____

How you treat yourself:
_____

How you feel about yourself:
_____

What's different in your life:
_____

Your Sacred Contract

I, _____,
commit to:
- Showing up daily, even imperfectly
- Being honest in my reflections
- Practicing self-compassion when I struggle
- Celebrating small wins
- Trusting the process
- Returning without judgment if I drift

My Personal Why:
_____
_____
_____
_____
_____

Signature: _____
Date: _____
Witness (optional): _____

Returning With Compassion

Missing days doesn't mean failure. Life happens.
What matters is your return.

If You've Missed

1-2 DAYS — Simply continue where you left off. No catch-up needed. Mark the missed days with a heart symbol (♡) to show self-compassion, then move forward.

3-5 DAYS
- Read through what you missed without doing all exercises
- Complete today's full practice
- Note any insights from your time away
- Continue with the current day

6-10 DAYS
- Return to the start of your current week
- Do a modified version: just morning intentions and evening gratitudes
- Focus on rebuilding the habit before adding complexity
- Be extra gentle with yourself

MORE THAN 10 DAYS
- Consider this a brave restart, not a failure
- Return to Week 1, Day 1 with all your new awareness
- Move through faster if content feels familiar
- Celebrate the courage to begin again

The Return Ritual

1. Place hand on heart
2. Say: "I'm exactly where I need to be"
3. Write: "Today I choose to return because _____"
4. Do one small practice (even 2 minutes counts)
5. Acknowledge your courage

Remember

- 100 imperfect days are better than 10 perfect ones
- Every return strengthens resilience
- You're not starting over; you're starting with experience
- The journal will always welcome you back

Common Return Blocks

- "I've ruined it" → You've learned what interrupts practice
- "I should start over" → You can build on what you know
- "I'm not committed enough" → You're here now; that's commitment
- "It's been too long" → There's no expiration date on self-love

Your Permission Slip

"I give myself complete permission to return to my practice at any time, without guilt, shame, or self-punishment. My journey is unique and valid."

Your Daily Practice Guide

Recommended Schedule

Foundation Phase (Days 1-30):
- 15-20 minutes daily
- Read one section every 6 days
- Complete activities at your pace
- Practice daily exercises

Practice Phase (Days 31-90):
- 10-15 minutes daily (or 2-3 minute minimum)
- Morning intention (5 min)
- Evening reflection (5 min)
- Weekly review on Sundays

Integration Phase (Days 87-90):
- 10 minutes daily
- Consolidation exercises
- Future planning
- Celebration activities

Essential Guidelines

1. Write Honestly
This is your private space. Write what's true, not what sounds good.

2. Progress Over Perfection
Missing a day doesn't mean failure. Return with kindness.

3. Adapt as Needed
Use practice options that fit your energy and schedule.

4. Trust the Process
Some days will feel repetitive. That's where neural rewiring happens.

Practical Tips:
- **Keep your journal accessible** - Visibility increases consistency
- **Set a phone reminder** - Same time daily builds habit
- **Use a special pen** - Make it feel ceremonial
- **Take progress photos** - Document your journey
- **Share with someone** - Accountability helps

When Resistance Arises:
Resistance is normal and expected. When it appears:
1. Acknowledge it without judgment
2. Do the minimum practice (2-3 minutes)
3. Remind yourself why you started
4. Be curious about what it's protecting
5. Continue anyway

You're Ready.
You have everything you need. The journey of 90 days begins with Day 1.
Trust yourself. Trust the process.

Begin Foundation Phase ⟶

WAIT! Before You Begin Day 1...

Get Your FREE Self-Love Support Toolkit (Worth $47!)

You're about to start something brave – transforming your inner critic into your biggest supporter. **Don't do it alone.**

We've created FREE resources specifically for where you are RIGHT NOW:

- ✓ **Day 1-30 Guided Meditations** – A calming voice for difficult moments
- ✓ **Emergency Self-Compassion Kit** – When the critic gets loud
- ✓ **Progress Trackers** – See your growth in real numbers
- ✓ **Daily Affirmations** – Replace criticism with kindness
- ✓ **"Return with Love" Worksheets** – For when you miss days

Scan now – setup takes 30 seconds

You deserve support. It's FREE. Get it now.

http://store.thedailywellness.com/freeselflovegifts

P.S. Readers who use the toolkit are 3x more likely to complete all 90 days. Give yourself every advantage – you're worth it.

Self-Criticism: Transforming Your Inner Dialogue

Section 1 of Your Foundation • Days 1-6

"The way you speak to yourself matters. Your inner dialogue becomes your inner reality."

What You'll Discover:

- Why your brain defaults to criticism
- The hidden patterns keeping you stuck
- Science-backed techniques for change
- How to become your own compassionate ally
- A sustainable practice for lasting transformation

Duration: Days 1-6
Daily commitment: 15-20 minutes

What Is Self-Criticism?

Self-criticism is the practice of harsh self-judgment, negative internal dialogue, and excessive focus on perceived inadequacies It's the voice that says you're not enough, no matter what you achieve.

Where Your Inner Critic Was Born

Early Experiences: High parental expectations • Conditional love • Comparison to siblings/peers • Academic/social struggles • Criticism from authority figures

Cultural Messages: Perfectionist standards • Social media comparisons • "Never satisfied" mentality • Productivity as worth

Protective Mechanisms: Avoiding disappointment • Preventing rejection • Maintaining control • Seeking connection

Impact on Your Wellbeing

Mental Health:
Increased anxiety, depression risk, low self-worth, rumination

Physical Health:
Chronic tension, sleep disruption, fatigue, headaches

Relationships:
Fear of intimacy, people-pleasing, poor boundaries, conflict avoidance

Life Satisfaction:
Reduced joy, limited growth, missed opportunities, chronic dissatisfaction

Common Patterns

PERSONALIZATION: "It's my fault" - Taking responsibility for things beyond your control

MAGNIFICATION: "This ruins everything" - Blowing mistakes out of proportion

LABELING: "I'm a failure" - Using harsh global judgments

ALL-OR-NOTHING: "Perfect or worthless" - Seeing only extremes

Quick Self-Assessment

Rate 1-5 (Never to Always)
- "I'm not good enough" _____
- "I should be further along" _____
- "I always mess things up" _____
- "Everyone else has it together" _____
- "What's wrong with me?" _____

Total: _____ / 25
(Higher scores = more self-criticism)

The Self-Criticism Cycle

- **TRIGGERS** (mistakes, comparisons, criticism)
- **THOUGHTS** ("I'm incompetent")
- **FEELINGS** (shame, anxiety)
- **BEHAVIORS** (withdrawal, procrastination)
- **PHYSICAL** (tension, fatigue)
- **REINFORCES BELIEFS**

Why We Criticize Ourselves

Despite its harmful effects, self-criticism serves psychological functions:

• UNREALISTIC STANDARDS •
The Perfectionist's Trap

We set impossible goals, then criticize ourselves for being human. Stems from childhood messages, fear of mediocrity, comparison culture.

• TRAUMA AND WOUNDS •
The Past Speaking

Unresolved experiences create critical inner voices through internalized criticism, self-blame as control, protective self-rejection.

• NEGATIVE CORE BELIEFS •
Hidden Programming

Deep beliefs about unworthiness: "I must earn love," "I'm fundamentally flawed," "I don't deserve good things."

The Neuroscience

When you criticize yourself:

Amygdala → Danger Signal → Cortisol → Stress Response → Fight/Flight → Survival Mode

This is why self-criticism feels so real and urgent – your brain treats it as an actual threat.

What Self-Criticism Really Does

DOESN'T:
- Make you perform better
- Protect from failure
- Help learn from mistakes
- Make others like you more
- Keep you safe

DOES:
- Activate stress response
- Impair decision-making
- Increase anxiety/depression
- Damage relationships
- Limit potential

6 Evidence-Based Strategies

1. Thought Stopping
Interrupt the pattern (Say "STOP" out loud, clap, take 3 breaths)

2. Cognitive Reframing
Challenge the thought (Is this 100% true? What would I tell a friend?)

3. Self-Compassion Break
Place hand on heart: "This is struggle. Struggle is human. May I be kind to myself."

4. Behavioral Activation
Act despite criticism (Do opposite, take imperfect action, focus on values)

5. Mindful Observation
Watch without attachment (Notice, label, let pass, return to present)

6. Gratitude Practice
Shift focus (3 things done well, 3 gratitudes, 1 self-appreciation, 1 growth moment)

The S.T.O.P. Technique

STOP: Pause and breathe. Create space between you and the thought.

THINK: Is this based on facts? Would I say this to someone I love?

OBSERVE: Notice body feelings, emotions, intensity (1-10), triggers.

PROCEED: Choose your response - compassion, reframe, caring action, support.

ACTIVITY – IDENTIFY & TRANSFORM

Discovering Your Critic's Origins

Rate frequency in childhood (1-5):
- Being compared to others: _____
- Receiving conditional love: _____
- Hearing "not good enough": _____
- Perfectionist expectations: _____
- Criticism for mistakes: _____

Whose voice does your inner critic sound like? _____
_____

Family Messages About:
- Success: _____
- Failure: _____
- Worth: _____

The core fear behind my criticism: _____
My critic is trying to protect me from: _____

Identifying Your Triggers

Check your top triggers & rate intensity (1-5):

- ☐ Morning Routine _____
- ☐ Work Meetings _____
- ☐ Social Media _____
- ☐ Appearance _____
- ☐ Messages _____
- ☐ Performance Reviews _____
- ☐ Relationships _____
- ☐ Family _____
- ☐ Finances _____
- ☐ Creative Work _____

Environmental changes I can make: _____
_____

ACTIVITY - CREATE YOUR SAFE SPACE

Physical Safe Space

Where feels most peaceful? _____
_____

What would make it more nurturing?

- ☐ Soft Lighting
- ☐ Comfortable Seating
- ☐ Plants
- ☐ Calming Colors
- ☐ Meaningful Objects
- ☐ Music
- ☐ Aromatherapy
- ☐ Journal

Mental Safe Space

Visualize a place criticism cannot reach:
- What you see: _____
- What you hear: _____
- How you feel: _____

Your Support Network

Inner Circle (1-3 most trusted):
1. Name: _____ How they help: _____
2. Name: _____ How they help: _____
3. Name: _____ How they help: _____

Self-Soothing Toolkit
- Physical: (bath, walk, yoga) _____
- Creative: (music, art, writing) _____
- Social: (friend, pet) _____
- Spiritual: (meditation, nature) _____

ACTIVITY – SHIFTING YOUR SELF-TALK

Transform Critical Language

Critical Language	Compassionate Alternative
"I'm such an idiot"	"I'm learning and growing"
"I always mess up"	"Sometimes I make mistakes"
"I'm not good enough"	I'm doing my best"
"What's wrong with me?"	"What do I need right now?"
Your phrase:	You rewrite:

The Compassionate Friend Technique

Someone you deeply care about: _____
What would you tell them if they made your mistake?
_____
_____

Now say this to yourself.

Daily Reframe Practice

MORNING
Critical Thought: Compassionate Reframe:
_____   →   _____
_____   _____

AFTERNOON
Critical Thought: Compassionate Reframe:
_____   →   _____
_____   _____

EVENING
Critical Thought: Compassionate Reframe:
_____   →   _____
_____   _____

Your Compassion Phrases:
1. _____
2. _____
3. _____

Days 1-6 Practice Guide

DAY 1: Awareness Without Judgment
"Today I observe my inner critic with curiosity, not judgment."

Tracking Log:
- Morning Time _____ Thought: _____ Trigger: _____
- Afternoon Time _____ Thought: _____ Trigger: _____
- Evening Time _____ Thought: _____ Trigger: _____

Patterns Noticed: _____ Critic Loudest When: _____

DAY 2: Applying S.T.O.P.
"Today I practice pausing and choosing compassion."

Use S.T.O.P. 3 times. Note what happened: _____

DAY 3: Integration & Reframing
"Today I actively transform criticism into compassion."

Practice reframing every critical thought. Note breakthrough moments:
_____

DAY 4: The Friend Perspective
"Today I speak to myself as I would to someone I love."

Friend voice responses: _____

DAY 5: Building New Pathways
"Each kind thought creates a stronger pathway to self-love."

New thought practiced: _____

DAY 6: Integration & Celebration
"I celebrate transforming my inner dialogue."

Six days complete! Key insights: _____

Section Integration Checklist

Rate yourself (1-10):
- I notice self-critical thoughts: Before: _____ Now: _____
- I can interrupt the cycle: Before: _____ Now: _____
- I practice self-compassion: Before: _____ Now: _____

Key Insights:
- My biggest revelation: _____
- Technique that works best: _____
- Pattern I'm releasing: _____

Your Certificate of Progress

I, _____, have completed the Self-Criticism section. I've learned to recognize patterns, interrupt the cycle, and choose compassion.
Date: _____

Ready for Self-Neglect Section? ☐ Yes ☐ Need more practice

Remember: This is your journey. Move at your pace. Every step forward matters.

Section 2: Self-Neglect (Days 7-12) →

Self-Neglect: Reclaiming Your Worth

Section 2 of Your Foundation • Days 7-12

"You cannot pour from an empty cup. Self-care is not selfish—it's essential."

What You'll Discover:

- Why we abandon ourselves and our needs
- The hidden costs of chronic self-neglect
- How to identify your neglect patterns
- Evidence-based self-care strategies
- Building a sustainable wellness practice

Duration: Days 7-12
Daily commitment: 15-20 minutes

What Is Self-Neglect?

Self-neglect is the behavioral pattern of consistently failing to meet your own physical, emotional, and psychological needs while often prioritizing others' needs or external demands above your own wellbeing.

The Many Faces of Self-Neglect

Learned Patterns: Childhood emotional neglect • "Others first" messaging • Punishment for needs • Praise for self-sacrifice

Emotional Neglect: Suppressing feelings • Avoiding joy • Denying need for comfort • Refusing self-compassion • Isolating when hurting

Mental Neglect: Constant overwork • No mental breaks • Ignoring stress signals • Avoiding help • Denying rest needs

Social Neglect: Isolation from loved ones • Refusing support • Toxic relationships • Avoiding connection • No boundaries

Root Causes

Learned Patterns:
Childhood emotional neglect • "Others first" messaging • Punishment for needs • Praise for self-sacrifice

Core Beliefs:
"My needs don't matter" • "I'm not worth the effort" • "Others are more important" • "Needing help is weakness"

Life Circumstances:
Chronic stress/burnout • Caregiver responsibilities • Depression/anxiety • Trauma responses • Overwhelming demands

The Cost of Self-Neglect

Immediate Impact	Long-term Consequences
Exhaustion, irritability	Chronic health issues
Poor concentration	Relationship breakdown
Mood swings	Career burnout
Physical symptoms	Depression/anxiety
Resentment	Loss of identity

Quick Self-Assessment

Rate 1-5 (Never to Always)
- Put others' needs first: _____
- Skip meals when busy: _____
- Ignore emotional needs: _____
- Feel guilty for self-care: _____
- Push through exhaustion: _____

Total: _____ / 25
(Higher scores = more self-neglect)

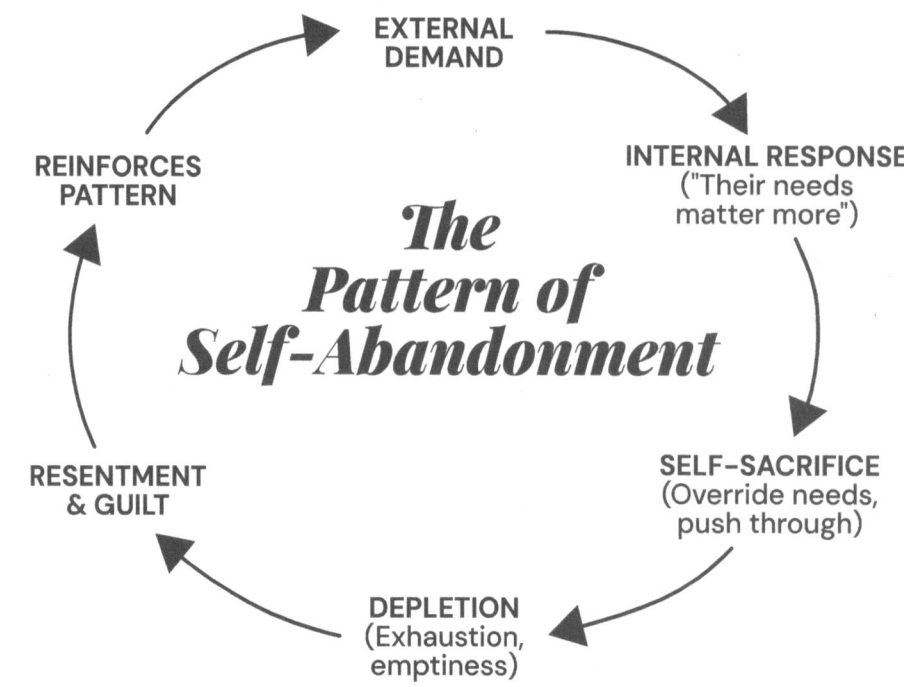

The Pattern of Self-Abandonment

- EXTERNAL DEMAND
- INTERNAL RESPONSE ("Their needs matter more")
- SELF-SACRIFICE (Override needs, push through)
- DEPLETION (Exhaustion, emptiness)
- RESENTMENT & GUILT
- REINFORCES PATTERN

Three Types of Self-Abandonment

SELF-BETRAYAL
Breaking Promises to Yourself
Saying yes when you mean no, Ignoring intuition, Compromising values, Hiding feelings, Accepting less than you deserve

Internal Message: "What I want doesn't matter"

PEOPLE-PLEASING
Trading Authenticity for Acceptance
Constant accommodation, Fear of disappointing, Excessive apologizing, Conflict avoidance, Shape-shifting for approval

Internal Message: "I'm only valuable when useful"

SELF-SACRFICE
Martyrdom as Identity
Always the "strong one", Never asking for help, Giving until depleted, Pride in suffering, Resenting others' needs

Internal Message: "My suffering proves my worth"

Why This Cycle Persists

Secondary Gains (What self-neglect provides):
Avoiding others' disappointment • Feeling needed • Avoiding emotions • Sense of control • Identity as "helper"

Fear of Change (What keeps us stuck):
Fear of being seen as selfish • Fear of rejection • Fear of not being needed • Fear of facing own needs • Fear of others' anger

Energy Balance Check

- Energy spent on others: _____ %
- Energy kept for self: _____ %
- Daily hours for others: _____
- Daily hours for self: _____

ACTIVITY – EVALUATE & END SELF-NEGLECT

Self-Neglect Inventory

Check all that apply:

Physical
- ☐ Skip meals
- ☐ Dehydrated
- ☐ Sacrifice sleep
- ☐ Ignore pain
- ☐ Forget medications
- ☐ No exercise
- ☐ Quick eating
- ☐ Work through exhaustion

Emotional
- ☐ Suppress feelings
- ☐ Don't cry
- ☐ Minimize struggles
- ☐ Avoid comfort
- ☐ Deny needs
- ☐ Isolate
- ☐ No celebrating
- ☐ Avoid joy

Mental
- ☐ Never take breaks
- ☐ Constant multitasking
- ☐ Ignore stress
- ☐ Negative content
- ☐ Don't protect peace
- ☐ Avoid learning
- ☐ Ruminate
- ☐ Deny help

Social
- ☐ Draining relationships
- ☐ Doesn't reach out
- ☐ No boundaries
- ☐ Cancels self-care plans
- ☐ Accepts poor treatment
- ☐ Doesn't express needs
- ☐ Gives more than receives

Areas with most checkmarks: 1. _____ 2. _____

Identifying Your Patterns

When do you neglect yourself most?
- Time of day: _____
- Situations: _____
- With whom: _____
- Emotional states: _____

Your Self-Neglect Triggers (Rate 1-5):
- Work demands: _____
- Family needs: _____
- Relationships: _____
- Financial stress: _____
- Conflict: _____
- Others' emotions: _____

When I neglect myself, I'm trying to:
- ☐ Avoid conflict
- ☐ Earn love
- ☐ Feel valuable
- ☐ Maintain control
- ☐ Avoid feelings
- ☐ Prevent abandonment

Your Warning Signs
- Physical: _____
- Emotional: _____
- Behavioral: _____

ACTIVITY – WELLNESS GOALS & HEALING

Creating Your Self-Care Vision

Physical Wellness
Current State: _____ ⟶ Desired State: _____
3 Goals:
1. _____
2. _____
3. _____

Emotional Wellness
Current State: _____ ⟶ Desired State: _____
3 Goals:
1. _____
2. _____
3. _____

Mental Wellness
Current State: _____ ⟶ Desired State: _____
3 Goals:
1. _____
2. _____
3. _____

Reconnecting Your Needs

Rate how well you meet each need (1-5):

- Physical safety: _____
- Rest/Sleep: _____
- Nutrition: _____
- Movement: _____
- Touch/Comfort: _____
- Medical care: _____

- Emotional safety: _____
- Expression: _____
- Validation: _____
- Connection: _____
- Joy/Play: _____
- Peace: _____

Identifying Your Patterns

Internal:
- ☐ Guilt
- ☐ Shame
- ☐ Fear of selfishlessness
- ☐ Not knowing how
- ☐ Feeling undeserving
- ☐ Perfectionism

External:
- ☐ Time constraints
- ☐ Financial limits
- ☐ Others' expectations
- ☐ Work demands
- ☐ Family responsiblities
- ☐ Lack of support

Your Healing Statement

"I acknowledge that I have been neglecting _____ . This pattern developed because _____ . I am ready to heal by _____ . I deserve care because _____ ."

ACTIVITY - INVEST IN YOU

Building Your Self-Care Practice

Morning Rituals (Choose 3):
- ☐ Gentle stretching
- ☐ Mindful breathing
- ☐ Gratitude
- ☐ Nourishing breakfast
- ☐ Inspiring reading
- ☐ Setting intentions
- ☐ Skincare
- ☐ Morning walk

Workday Boundaries:
- ☐ Lunch breaks (non-negotiable)
- ☐ Breathing breaks hourly
- ☐ Standing/stretching
- ☐ Limiting overtime
- ☐ Saying no
- ☐ Protected focus time

Evening Rituals (Choose 3):
- ☐ Tech cutoff
- ☐ Calming tea
- ☐ Gentle movement
- ☐ Reading
- ☐ Bath/shower ritual
- ☐ Journaling
- ☐ Prep for tomorrow
- ☐ Early bedtime

Your Support Team
- Doctor: _____
- Therapist: _____
- Emergency contact: _____
- Check-in buddy: _____
- Accountability partner: _____

Investment Calculator

Time I'll invest in self-care daily: _____ minutes
Energy this will save me: _____ %
How this improves my life: _____

Weekly Self-Care Appointment
Day: _____ Time: _____ Activity: _____
Non-negotiable? YES ☐

Your Wellness Commitment

"I commit to treating my needs as valid and important. Starting today, I will honor my wellbeing by:"

- Daily: _____
- Weekly: _____
- Monthly: _____

Signature: _____ Date: _____

Days 7-9 Practice Guide

DAY 7: Awareness of Neglect
"Today I notice when and how I abandon my own needs."

Check-in Log:
- Morning Needs:
  Body: _____ Emotions: _____ Mind: _____

- Did I honor these? ☐ Yes ☐ No

- Afternoon:
  What needs am I ignoring? _____ Why? _____

- Evening
  Times I chose others over myself: _____ How it felt: _____

DAY 8: Setting Boundaries
"Today I practice saying yes to myself and no to depletion."

Boundary Practice:
- Boundary 1: Situation: _____
  What I did: _____ How it felt: _____

- Boundary 2: Situation: _____
  What I did: _____ How it felt: _____

- Boundary 3: Situation: _____
  What I did: _____ How it felt: _____

DAY 9: Active Self-Care
"Today I actively invest in my wellbeing."

Care Provided:
- Physical: _____
- Emotional: _____
- Mental: _____
- Social: _____

Days 10-12 Practice Guide

DAY 10: Meeting Basic Needs
"Today I honor my fundamental requirements for wellbeing."

Basic Needs Met:
- ☐ Adequate sleep (hours: _____)
- ☐ Three meals
- ☐ Water (glasses: _____)
- ☐ Movement (minutes: _____)
- ☐ Rest breaks
- ☐ Connection

Reflection:
Meeting my needs felt: _____

DAY 11: Guilt-Free Self-Care
"Today I practice self-care without apology."

Self-Care Without Guilt:
- What I did for myself: _____

- Guilt level (1-10): _____
- How I managed guilt: _____

- What I'm learning: _____

DAY 12: Integration & Celebration
"I celebrate reclaiming my worth through self-care."

Six Days of Self-Care:
- Biggest insight: _____

- Most helpful practice: _____

- Pattern I'm changing: _____

- Commitment going forward: _____

Section Integration Checklist

Rate yourself (1-10):
- I recognize self-neglect:
  Before: _____ Now: _____
- I can set boundaries:
  Before: _____ Now: _____
- I practice self-care:
  Before: _____ Now: _____

Key Insights:
- My biggest revelation: _____

- Self-care practice that works best: _____

- Pattern I'm changing: _____

Your Self-Care Protocol

Daily Non-Negotiables:
- Morning: _____

- Afternoon: _____

- Evening: _____

Weekly Wellness: _____
_____
_____

Your Certificate of Progress

I, _____, have completed the Self-Neglect section. I've learned to recognize my patterns, honor my needs, and commit to ongoing self-care.

Date: _____

Ready for Self-Acceptance Section? ☐ Yes ☐ Need more practice

Remember: Your needs matter. Meeting them isn't selfish—it's necessary.

Section 3: Self-Acceptance (Days 13-18) ⟶

Self-Acceptance: Embracing Your Whole Self

Section 3 of Your Foundation • Days 13-18

"To be beautiful means to be yourself. You don't need to be accepted by others. You need to accept yourself."

What You'll Discover:

- The true meaning of self-acceptance
- Why acceptance differs from resignation
- How to embrace all parts of yourself
- Building lasting self-appreciation

Duration: Days 13-18
Daily commitment: 15-20 minutes

What Is Self-Acceptance?

Self-acceptance is embracing all aspects of yourself—strengths, weaknesses, successes, and failures—without harsh judgment. It's recognizing your inherent value regardless of achievements.

The 4 Components

1 **Awareness** – *Seeing Yourself Clearly*
Observing thoughts and patterns with curiosity, not criticism.

2 **Self-Compassion** – *Responding with Kindness*
Treating yourself as you would a good friend.

3 **Empowerment** – *Owning Your Story*
Taking responsibility while knowing worth isn't determined by achievements.

4 **Embracing Imperfection** – *Owning Your Story*
Understanding flaws don't diminish your value.

Impact on Life

Mental Health:
- Reduced anxiety
- Lower stress
- Better emotional regulation

Relationships:
- Authentic connections
- Better boundaries
- Deeper intimacy

Personal Growth:
- Freedom to take risks
- Learning from mistakes
- Creative expression

Life Satisfaction:
- Increased joy
- Present-moment awareness
- Greater fulfillment

Quick Self-Assessment

Rate your acceptance level (1-10):
- Physical appearance: _____
- Personality traits: _____
- Past decisions: _____
- Emotions: _____
- Limitations: _____

Total: _____ / 50

Common Acceptance Blocks

FEAR OF COMPLACENCY
"If I accept myself, I'll never improve"
Truth: Acceptance provides stable foundation for growth

PERFECTIONIST PROGRAMMING
"I'll accept myself when I'm good enough"
Truth: Worth isn't earned; it's inherent

COMPARISON CULTURE
"Everyone else seems better"
Truth: Your journey is unique and valuable

PAST WOUNDS
"I've been told I'm not enough"
Truth: Old messages don't define your worth

6 Steps to Self-Acceptance

1. **ACKNOWLEDGE REALITY** — See what is without filters
2. **RELEASE JUDGMENT** — Replace criticism with curiosity
3. **PRACTICE COMPASSION** — Speak kindly to yourself
4. **HONOR YOUR JOURNEY** — Recognize how far you've come
5. **EMBRACE WHOLENESS** — Accept all parts of you
6. **COMMIT TO PRACTICE** — Make acceptance daily

Your Acceptance Blockers

Check all that apply:
- ☐ Perfectionist standards
- ☐ Past criticism voices
- ☐ Cultural expectations
- ☐ Comparison to others
- ☐ Fear of judgment
- ☐ Family messages

Strongest blocker: _____

One step to release it: _____

ACTIVITY – EMBRACING YOUR WHOLE SELF

Acceptance Inventory

Parts I Need to Accept More:
- Physical: _____
- Emotional: _____
- Mental: _____
- Past choices: _____

Parts I'm Proud Of:
1. _____
2. _____
3. _____

The Both/And Practice
Complete these statements:
- "I am both _____ and _____"
- "I am both _____ and _____"
- "I am both _____ and _____"

Example: "I am both strong and vulnerable"

Your Identity Map

How I See Myself:
- Strengths: _____
- Challenges: _____
- Growth Areas: _____

How Others See Me:
- Family says: _____
- Friends say: _____
- I'm surprised when: _____

Acceptance Affirmations
Choose 3 that resonate:
- ☐ "I accept myself completely"
- ☐ "My imperfections make me unique"
- ☐ "I am worthy as I am"
- ☐ "I embrace my whole story"
- ☐ "I belong here"
- ☐ "My journey is valid"

Daily affirmation I'll use: _____

Days 13-15 Practice Guide

DAY 13: Awareness Without Judgment
"Today I observe myself with curiosity"

Morning Check-in:
What I notice about myself: _____

Without judgment, I see: _____

I appreciate: _____

Evening Reflection:
I accepted: _____

I struggled with: _____

Tomorrow I'll practice: _____

DAY 14: Embracing Imperfection
"Today I embrace one imperfection with kindness"

Morning Check-in:
Imperfection to embrace: _____

Kind reframe: _____

Evening Reflection:
How acceptance felt: _____

What shifted: _____

DAY 15: Practicing Wholeness
"Today I honor all parts of myself"

Morning Check-in:
Parts of me present today: _____

I welcome them because: _____

Evening Reflection:
I experienced wholeness when: _____

This taught me: _____

Days 16-18 Practice Guide

DAY 16: The Both/And Practice
"Today I embrace my contradictions"

Morning Practice:
I am both _____ and _____
This means I can: _____

Evening Reflection:
Contradictions I embraced: _____

Freedom I felt: _____

DAY 17: Radical Acceptance
"Today I accept what I cannot change"

Morning Practice:
What I cannot change: _____

How I can accept it: _____

Evening Reflection:
Acceptance brought: _____

Peace level (1-10): _____

DAY 18: Integration
"Today I celebrate my complete self"

Morning Practice:
I accept that I am: _____

My commitment to acceptance: _____

Evening Reflection:
My biggest breakthrough: _____

Moving forward, I will: _____

Section Integration

Progress Check
Rate yourself now (vs. Day 13):
- I accept my physical self:
  Before (1-10): _____ Now (1-10): _____
- I accept my emotions:
  Before (1-10): _____ Now (1-10): _____
- I accept my past:
  Before (1-10): _____ Now (1-10): _____
- I accept my limitations:
  Before (1-10): _____ Now (1-10): _____
- I accept my whole self:
  Before (1-10): _____ Now (1-10): _____

Key Insights:
- My biggest breakthrough: _____
  _____
  _____
- Practice that helped most: _____
  _____
  _____
- What I'm ready to accept: _____
  _____
  _____
- What needs more work: _____
  _____
  _____

Your Acceptance Declaration

"I, _____ , accept myself completely. I embrace my strengths and challenges, my light and shadow. I am worthy of love exactly as I am while remaining open to growth."

Date: _____

Daily practices I'll continue:
- ☐ Morning acceptance check-in
- ☐ Compassionate self-talk
- ☐ Evening appreciation
- ☐ Whole self-acknowledgement

Weekly ritual: _____

Your Certificate of Progress

I have completed the Self-Acceptance section. I've learned to embrace my whole self with awareness, compassion, and acceptance of my beautiful imperfections.

Ready for Self-Compassion Section? ☐ Yes ☐ Need more practice

Remember: Self-acceptance is a journey, not a destination.

Section 4: Self-Compassion (Days 19-24) ⟶

You're Halfway Through Your Foundation!

Incredible Work – But Are You Getting All The Support You Deserve?

You've spent 3 sections transforming self-criticism, ending self-neglect, and building self-acceptance. That takes COURAGE.

If you haven't grabbed your FREE toolkit yet, now's the perfect time.

The next sections (Self-Compassion & Self-Love) can bring up deep emotions. Don't face them without support:

What's Waiting for You (FREE):

- ✓ **Compassion Meditations** for when it gets intense
- ✓ **Progress Tracker** to see how far you've actually come
- ✓ **Breakthrough Worksheets** for stuck moments
- ✓ **Emergency Comfort Kit** for overwhelming days
- ✓ **Community of 100,000+** walking this path with you

Scan now – even if you think you don't need it
(You will on Day 37, 52, or 73... trust us)

Already got it? Amazing!
Haven't yet? No judgment – just get it now. You've earned it.
http://store.thedailywellness.com/freeselflovegifts

Real talk: The second half of this journey goes deeper. Having meditation audios on your phone for emergency moments isn't "nice to have" – it's essential. Get your FREE support now.

Self-Compassion: Treating Yourself With Kindness

Section 4 of Your Foundation • Days 19-24

"Talk to yourself like you would to someone you love."

What You'll Discover:

- The three elements of self-compassion
- Why kindness toward yourself matters
- How to break harsh self-treatment cycles
- Building a sustainable compassion habit

Duration: Days 19-24
Daily commitment: 15-20 minutes

What Is Self-Compassion?

Self-compassion is treating yourself with the same kindness and support you'd show a good friend, especially during failure or suffering. It recognizes imperfection as part of being human.

The Three Core Elements

1. SELF-KINDNESS vs. SELF-JUDGMENT
Offering warmth and understanding instead of harsh criticism.

- *Self-Judgment: "I'm stupid for this mistake"*
- *Self-Kindness: "Everyone makes mistakes. What can I learn?"*

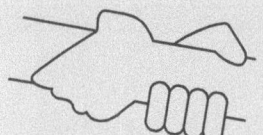

2. COMMON HUMANITY vs. ISOLATION
Recognizing suffering as universal, not unique to you.

- *Isolation: "I'm the only one who struggles"*
- *Common Humanity: "This is part of being human"*

3. MINDFULNESS vs. OVER-IDENTIFICATION
Observing difficult feelings without becoming consumed.

- *Over-identification: "Everything is ruined!"*
- *Mindfulness: "This is a moment of difficulty"*

Benefits of Self-Compassion

Research shows it:
- Reduces anxiety/depression by 50%
- Increases motivation and growth
- Improves relationships
- Enhances resilience
- Boosts immune function
- Promotes better sleep

Quick Self-Assessment

Rate how often you (1-5):
- Treat yourself kindly when failing: _____
- Remember others struggle too: _____
- Give yourself comfort: _____
- Notice suffering without drama: _____
- Forgive your mistakes: _____

Total: _____ / 25

Practicing the 3 Components

Component 1: Self-Kindness

When You Make a Mistake:
1. Acknowledge without attacking
2. Ask "What would I tell a friend?"
3. Focus on learning and growth

Your Kindness Phrase:
"When I struggle, I will tell myself:
_____"

Component 2: Common Humanity

Remember:
- Everyone fails sometimes
- Perfection is impossible
- Mistakes are universal
- You're not alone

Your Connection Reminder:
"When I feel alone, I'll remember:
_____"

Component 3: Mindfulness

How to Practice:
- Notice emotions without judgment
- Observe thoughts as temporary
- Stay present with feelings
- Return to breath

Your Mindfulness Anchor:
"When overwhelmed, I'll:
_____"

The Self-Compassion Break

When struggling, place hand on heart and say:
1. "This is a moment of suffering"
2. "Suffering is part of life"
3. "May I be kind to myself"
4. "May I give myself compassion"

Practice Scenario

Situation: _____

Without compassion: _____

With compassion: _____

ACTIVITY – COMPASSION IN ACTION

Letter to Your Struggling Self

Dear _____ ,

I see that you're struggling with: _____

This is hard because: _____

I want you to know: _____

You're not alone in this because: _____

What you need to hear right now: _____
_____

I'm here for you and will: _____

With love and compassion,

_____

Transform Critical Thoughts

Critical Thought	Compassionate Response
"I always mess up"	"Sometimes I make mistakes, and that's okay"
"I'm not good enough"	"I'm doing my best with what I know"
"What's wrong with me?"	"I'm human and learning"
Your phrase:	Your response:
Your phrase:	Your response:

Daily Compassion Phrases

Create personal phrases for:

When I make a mistake: " _____ "

When I feel inadequate: " _____ "

When I'm struggling: " _____ "

Days 19-21 Practice Guide

DAY 19: Recognizing Suffering
"Today I acknowledge my struggles with kindness"

Morning Check-in:
Current struggles: _____

I acknowledge this is difficult because: _____

Evening Reflection:
I recognized suffering when: _____

I offered myself: _____

Self-Compassion Break:
☐ Practiced today

DAY 20: Common Humanity
"Today I remember I'm not alone"

Morning Check-in:
A challenge I face: _____

Others who understand: _____

Evening Reflection:
I felt connected when: _____

This helped me realize: _____

Connection Practice:
"Just like me, others feel _____ "

DAY 21: Offering Kindness
"Today I speak to myself as a friend"

Morning Check-in:
If my friend felt this way, I'd say: _____

So I tell myself: _____

Evening Reflection:
Kind words I offered: _____

This felt: _____

Days 22-24 Practice Guide

DAY 22: Mindful Awareness
"Today I observe without over-identifying"

Morning Check-in:
Difficult feeling present: _____

I can observe it without: _____

Evening Reflection:
Mindfulness helped when: _____

Distance created: _____

DAY 23: Self-Compassion in Action
"Today I take caring actions"

Morning Check-in:
What I need today: _____

How I'll provide it: _____

Evening Reflection:
I cared for myself by: _____

Impact on wellbeing: _____

DAY 24: Integration
"Today I celebrate growing compassion"

Morning Check-in:
Six days of compassion taught me: _____

My commitment: _____

Evening Reflection:
My biggest shift: _____

Going forward: _____

Section Integration

Progress Check
Rate yourself now (vs. Day 19):
- I treat myself kindly:
  Before (1-10): _____ Now (1-10): _____
- I remember shared humanity:
  Before (1-10): _____ Now (1-10): _____
- I practice mindfulness:
  Before (1-10): _____ Now (1-10): _____
- I offer comfort:
  Before (1-10): _____ Now (1-10): _____
- I forgive mistakes:
  Before (1-10): _____ Now (1-10): _____

Key Insights:
- My biggest shift: _____

- Most helpful practice: _____

- Critical voice that softened: _____

- How I'll maintain compassion: _____

Your Self-Compassion Toolkit

Daily practices I'll continue:
- ☐ Morning compassion break
- ☐ Kind inner dialogue
- ☐ Evening gratitude
- ☐ Compassionate touch

Emergency Compassion Plan:

When struggling, I will:
1. Place hand on heart
2. Say "This is hard right now"
3. Remember "I'm not alone"
4. Offer "May I be kind to myself"
5. Ask "What do I need?"

My Compassion Pledge

"I, _____ , pledge to treat myself with compassion. I will speak to myself as I would a dear friend and offer myself the kindness I deserve."

Date: _____

Your Certificate of Progress

I have completed the Self-Compassion section. I've learned to recognize suffering, embrace common humanity, and offer myself kindness.

Ready for Self-Love Section? ☐ Yes   ☐ Need more practice

Remember: Self-compassion is a practice, not perfection.

Section 5: Self-Love (Days 25-30) →

Self-Love: The Foundation of Your Worth

Section 5 of Your Foundation • Days 25-30

"Your relationship with yourself sets the tone for every other relationship you have."

What You'll Discover:

- The true meaning of self-love
- The 5 essential components
- Breaking through love-blocking barriers
- Creating your personal love language

Duration: Days 25-30
Daily commitment: 15-20 minutes

What Is Self-Love?

Self-love is valuing, respecting, and caring for yourself as a whole person. It means recognizing your inherent worth and treating yourself with the same care you'd give someone precious.

Self-Love IS vs. IS NOT

Self-Love IS:	Self-Love IS NOT:
Recognizing inherent worth	Narcissism or superiority
Meeting your needs	Harming others
Setting boundaries	Ignoring growth
Celebrating uniqueness	Constant indulgence
Forgiving mistakes	Isolation
Prioritizing wellbeing	Perfection

The 5 Components

1 Self-Awareness
Knowing your values, needs, triggers, strengths, and dreams.
Your awareness level (1-10): _____

2 Self-Worth
Believing you deserve love, respect, and good things.
Your worth level (1-10): _____

3 Self-Care
Actively nurturing your physical, emotional, mental, and spiritual self.
Your care level (1-10): _____

4 Self-Respect
Maintaining boundaries, standards, and authentic expression.
Your respect level (1-10): _____

5 Self-Trust
Having faith in your decisions, judgment, and resilience.
Your trust level (1-10): _____

Total Self-Love Score: _____ /50

Foundation of Confidence

Self-love builds confidence through:

- **Internal validation** - Worth comes from within
- **Risk-taking ability** - Self-support through failure
- **Authentic expression** - Accepting all parts
- **Resilience** - Being your own ally
- **Healthy relationships** - Knowing your worth

Common Self-Love Blocks

INNER CRITIC
"You don't deserve love"
Response: "This is old programming I can change"

PERFECTIONISM
"Must be flawless to be lovable"
Response: "I am worthy in my imperfection"

PAST WOUNDS
"Previous pain defines worth"
Response: "My past doesn't determine my value"

COMPARISON TRAP
"Others are better"
Response: "My journey is unique and valuable"

Your Self-Love Blocks

Check all that apply:
- ☐ "I need to earn love"
- ☐ "Self-love is selfish"
- ☐ "I'm not worthy yet"
- ☐ "Others deserve it more"
- ☐ "I don't know how"

Primary block: _____
One step to release it: _____

6 Benefits of Self-Love

1. Mental Health
Reduced anxiety, increased happiness

2. Relationships
Healthier boundaries, authentic connections

3. Confidence
Belief in abilities, courage to risk

4. Physical Health
Better self-care, reduced stress

5. Success
Pursuing dreams, resilience through setbacks

6. Authentic Living
Following truth, expressing uniqueness

Which benefit motivates you most? _____

― Daily Self-Love Practice ―

The S.E.L.F. Technique

S – SUPPORT YOURSELF

Be Your Own Best Friend
- Encourage through challenges
- Celebrate wins
- Comfort when hurting
- Trust decisions

Morning ask: "How can I support myself today?"
My answer: _____

E – EMBRACE YOUR TRUTH

Accept All of You
- Honor feelings
- Accept imperfections
- Express authenticity
- Acknowledge needs

Morning ask: "What truth needs embracing?"
My answer: _____

L – LOVE ACTIVELY

Take Loving Actions
- Practice self-care
- Set boundaries
- Choose nourishment
- Create joy

Morning ask: "What loving action will I take?"
My answer: _____

F – FORGIVE FREELY

Release and Renew
- Forgive mistakes
- Release regrets
- Let go of perfection
- Start fresh

Morning ask: "What needs forgiving?"
My answer: _____

― Creating Your Rituals ―

Morning (5 min):
1. Mirror moment with love
2. State one appreciation
3. Set loving intention
4. S.E.L.F. check-in

Evening (5 min):
1. Review day kindly
2. Acknowledge efforts
3. Forgive mistakes
4. Express gratitude

Days 25-27 Practice Guide

DAY 25: Self-Awareness
"Today I pay loving attention to myself"

Morning Check-in:
What I'm feeling: _____
What I need: _____
What brings joy: _____
What I value: _____

Evening Reflection:
I learned: _____
_____

I appreciate: _____
_____

DAY 26: Self-Worth
"Today I recognize my inherent value"

Morning Check-in:
I deserve love because: _____
I am worthy of: _____
My value comes from: _____

Evening Reflection:
I claimed worth through: _____
_____

This felt: _____

DAY 27: Self-Care
"Today I nurture myself lovingly"

Morning Check-in:
Body needs: _____
Heart needs: _____
Mind needs: _____
Spirit needs: _____

Care Actions:
- ☐ Physical: _____
- ☐ Emotional: _____
- ☐ Mental: _____
- ☐ Spiritual: _____

Days 28-30 Practice Guide

DAY 28: Self-Respect
"Today I honor my boundaries and values"

Morning Check-in:
My boundaries today: _____
My standards: _____
I will honor myself by: _____

Evening Reflection:
I maintained respect when: _____

This strengthened: _____

DAY 29: Self-Trust
"Today I trust my wisdom and resilience"

Morning Check-in:
I trust myself to: _____
My intuition says: _____
I have faith in: _____

Evening Reflection:
I trusted myself when: _____

This proved: _____

DAY 30: Integration
"Today I embody self-love fully"

Morning S.E.L.F.:
Support: _____
Embrace: _____
Love: _____
Forgive: _____

Evening Reflections:
Today's highlight: _____

My growth: _____

My commitment: _____

Congratulations!
Your Foundation Is Built!

Over 30 days, you have:
- Transformed self-criticism into awareness
- Ended self-neglect through self-care
- Embraced self-acceptance fully
- Cultivated self-compassion daily
- Activated self-love as practice

Foundation Assessment
Rate yourself Day 1 vs. Now (1-10):

Area	Day 1	Day 30	Growth
Self-Criticism	____	____	____
Self-Neglect	____	____	____
Self-Acceptance	____	____	____
Self-Compassion	____	____	____
Self-Love	____	____	____

Total Growth Points: _____

Your Transformation

When I started: _____
_____
_____

Now I am: _____
_____
_____

Biggest change: _____
_____
_____

Most proud of: _____
_____
_____

Daily Practices to Continue

Non-Negotiables:
- _____
- _____
- _____
- _____

Weekly Rituals:
- _____
- _____
- _____
- _____

Your Commitment Statement

"I, _____ , have built my foundation of self-love. I commit to continuing this journey with patience, kindness, and dedication. Self-love is a practice, not a destination."

Signature: _____
Date: _____

Foundation Certificate

This certifies that _____ has completed the Foundation Phase of their 90-Day Self-Love Breakthrough.

Date: _____

How will you celebrate? _____

Ready for the 60-Day Practice Journey?
☐ Yes   ☐ Need more practice   ☐ Rest day

Remember: You've done something remarkable. This foundation will support everything else you build in life.

30 Days Complete – YOU DID IT!

You've Built Your Foundation. Now Let's Build Your Future.

Take a moment. You just spent 30 days doing what most people never attempt – facing yourself with honesty and compassion. You're not the same person who started on Day 1.

The next 60 days are about making this transformation PERMANENT.

If you haven't claimed your FREE support toolkit yet, please do it now. Here's why:

Phase 2 is different. It's less structured, more self-directed. The days you'll want to quit are coming. The days you'll think "good enough" are ahead. That's normal – and that's why we created:

Your FREE Phase 2 Survival Kit: 30 Days of Audio Support
– Reusable meditations for every situation

- ✓ **Habit Tracking Templates**
  – Make self-love automatic
- ✓ **Reset Protocols**
  – For when old patterns return
- ✓ **Self-Love Cheat Sheets**
  – Quick wins for tough moments
- ✓ **Weekly Check-in Prompts**
  – Stay connected to your why

This is your last reminder. Get your FREE toolkit now.

"I made it 30 days without help" – Cool, but why make it harder?

"I already have it" – Perfect! Check your email for bonus Week 5 content.

http://store.thedailywellness.com/freeselflovegifts

Truth: Days 31–90 are where transformation becomes identity. You've proven you can start. Now let's make sure you finish. Get your FREE support and let's do this together.

P.S. – 87% of people who complete Day 30 WITHOUT the toolkit don't make it to Day 90. With it? 94% finish. Choose wisely.

From Learning to Living

You've built the foundation. Now it's time to live it.

Where You've Been

Over the past 30 days, you've learned five essential practices:

Self-Criticism → Awareness
You now notice critical thoughts and can interrupt them with compassion.

Self-Neglect → Self-Care
You recognize your needs and have tools to meet them.

Self-Acceptance → Wholeness
You're embracing all parts of yourself without harsh judgment.

Self-Compassion → Kindness
You treat yourself as you would a dear friend.

Self-Love → Worth
You recognize your inherent value and act from that knowing.

Where You're Going

The next 60 days transform knowledge into embodied practice. You'll:

Days 31-58:
Build daily awareness and consistency

Days 59-86:
Deepen your practice and integration

This isn't about perfection—it's about progress. Some days will feel easier than others. That's normal and expected.

Your Readiness Check

Before continuing, confirm:

- ☐ I understand this is a practice, not perfection
- ☐ I'm committed to showing up daily, even imperfectly
- ☐ I have self-compassion for difficult days
- ☐ I've celebrated completing my foundation
- ☐ I'm ready to deepen my self-love journey

If you checked all boxes: Continue to page 61
If you have hesitations: That's okay. Review any foundation section that needs strengthening.

A Personal Note

What you're doing takes courage. Choosing to love yourself in a world that profits from your self-doubt is revolutionary. Every day you practice, you're rewriting old patterns and creating new neural pathways. Trust the process.

YOUR PERSONALIZED PRACTICE PLAN ─────────

Designing Your Daily Practice

Your Optimal Practice Time
Morning person or night owl? Choose when you're most likely to succeed:

Morning Practice (Recommended)
- ☐ Upon waking (before phone)
- ☐ After morning routine
- ☐ With morning coffee/tea

Time: _____

Evening Practice
- ☐ After work
- ☐ Before dinner
- ☐ Before bed

Time: _____

Split Practice
- ☐ Brief morning (5 minutes)
- ☐ Full evening (10-15 minutes)

Times: _____ & _____

Your Practice Space

Designate a spot for your daily practice:
Location: _____
What makes it special: _____
_____

Items to keep there:
- ☐ This journal
- ☐ Favorite pen
- ☐ Candle or calming object
- ☐ Tea or water
- ☐ Tissues
- ☐ Other: _____

60 | Transition: From Learning to Living

Your Support System

Accountability Partner: _____
Check-in frequency: _____

Professional Support (if applicable):
Therapist/Coach: _____
Next appointment: _____

Community Support:
- ☐ Online group: _____
- ☐ Local group: _____
- ☐ Friend practicing: _____

CUSTOMIZING FOR YOUR LIFE

Your Current Life Season

Check what applies:
- ☐ High stress period
- ☐ Major transition
- ☐ Relatively stable
- ☐ Healing/Recovery
- ☐ Growth phase

Your Energy Level

Most days I have:
- ☐ High energy – Full practice
- ☐ Moderate energy – Standard practice
- ☐ Low energy – Minimum practice
- ☐ Variable – Flexible approach

Your Primary Focus Area

What needs most attention? (Pick 1-2)
- ☐ Critical inner voice
- ☐ Self-care habits
- ☐ Accepting myself
- ☐ Being kinder to myself
- ☐ Building self-worth

Your Practice Commitment

I commit to:
- ☐ Daily practice for 60 days
- ☐ Being honest in my reflections
- ☐ Celebrating small wins
- ☐ Forgiving missed days
- ☐ Returning when I drift

My minimum daily commitment: _____ minutes

What I hope to experience: _____

My why (what makes this matter): _____
_____

Signed: _____
Date: _____

62 | Transition: From Learning to Living

Tracking Your Progress

Weekly Check-ins (Sundays)

- Energy level (1-10): _____
- Consistency (days practiced): _____ /7
- Biggest insight: _____
- Next week's focus: _____

Monthly Milestone Rewards

- Day 60 reward: _____
- Day 90 celebration: _____

How To Use The Daily Pages

Each day in your 60-day journey includes specific elements designed to deepen self-love:

Daily Page Components

1 **Day & Date Counter**
Track your progress visually

2 **Daily Theme**
Each day has a focus

3 **Morning Practice (5-10 minutes)**
• Intention • Check-in • Gratitude • Focus

4 **Evening Reflection (5-10 minutes)**
• Wins • Challenges • Insights • Tomorrow

5 **Self-Love Tracker**
Rate daily (1-10)

Making It Sustainable

- Start where you are
- Progress, not perfection
- Missed days protocol (see page 11)
- Return with kindness

Ready?

Take a deep breath.
Place your hand on your heart.
Say "I choose me."
Turn the page.

Your 60-day practice begins now.

Continue to Day 31 ⟶

Transition: From Learning to Living | 63

Month 1: Building Awareness

Mindful Awareness
Days 31-37 of Your Practice

This week's focus: Building awareness of your thoughts, feelings, and patterns without judgment.

Mindful awareness is the foundation of all change. You can't transform what you don't notice. This week, you'll develop the skill of observing yourself with curiosity rather than criticism.

Week 1 Intentions

- Notice your inner dialogue without trying to change it
- Observe patterns in your thinking
- Practice being a neutral witness
- Build the awareness muscle
- Create space between you and your thoughts

Daily Structure This Week

Morning (5-10 min): Set intention, body scan, gratitude
During Day: Notice moments of self-talk
Evening (5-10 min): Reflect, track patterns, appreciate

Remember

There's no "perfect" way to do this. Simply noticing is enough. Awareness itself begins the transformation.

Support Reminder: If you experience distress during your practice, return to your support resources (Page 9) or reach out to a trusted friend or professional.

Practice Phase: Example Entry

Here's how Sarah filled out her Day 31 to guide your journey:

BUILDING AWARENESS ―――――――――――――――――

Date: _03_ / _15_ / _24_ • Practice Day 31 of 90

Morning Intention (2-5 minutes)

Today's Focus: Building Awareness

One Thing I'll Notice Today: _How often I apologize unnecessarily_

My Intention: _I observe myself with curiosity and kindness_

How I Want To Feel Tonight: _Proud that I noticed without judging_

Self-Check Scale (1-10):
Current mood: _6_ /10
Energy: _5_ /10
Self-compassion: _7_ /10

Evening Reflection

Awareness Noticed: _I said "sorry" 12 times for things that weren't my fault!_

Without Judgment: _I noticed this pattern comes from childhood - interesting!_

Tomorrow's Focus: _I'll try to pause before automatic apologies_

Celebrate: What Went Well?
I caught myself 3 times and didn't apologize!

Daily Tracking

☑ Morning Practice
☑ Evening Practice
Gentleness with self: _8_ /10

Tomorrow I Want to Notice:
My growing awareness - I'm finally seeing my patterns!

Note: Your entries can be shorter or longer - find what works for you!

BEGINNING WITH AWARENESS ─────────

Date: ___/___/___ • Practice Day 31 of 90

Today's Theme: *Starting Where You Are*

"The journey of a thousand miles begins with a single step."
Begin exactly where you are, not where you think you should be.

Morning Practice

Body Scan Check-in:
Head and neck: _____
Shoulders and chest: _____
Stomach and back: _____
Overall energy (1-10): _____

Today's Intention: "Today I will notice my thoughts with curiosity, not judgment."

Personal Addition: _____
_____
_____

Three Gratitudes: (This week: anything you appreciate)
1. _____
2. _____
3. _____

Awareness Prompts

What am I telling myself about starting this journey?
_____
_____
_____

What hope do I carry today?
_____
_____
_____

What fear needs acknowledgment?
_____
_____
_____

Evening Reflection

Moments I Noticed My Self-Talk:
Morning: _____
_____

Afternoon: _____
_____

Evening: _____
_____

Pattern I Observed: _____

Today's Wins: (Any size counts)
- ☐ Started this practice
- ☐ Noticed a thought pattern
- ☐ Paused before reacting
- ☐ Other: _____

One Thing I Learned:
_____
_____
_____

How I Showed Myself Love Today:
_____
_____
_____

Daily Tracking

Rate Your Day (1-10):
- Self-compassion: _____
- Overall awareness: _____
- Today's growth: _____

Tomorrow I Want to Notice:
_____
_____

Affirmation for Tonight:
"I completed Day 31. I showed up. That's enough."

OBSERVING WITHOUT JUDGMENT

Date: ___/___/___ • Day 32 of 90

Today's Theme: *The Neutral Observer*
Today, practice being a scientist studying your own mind.
Observe without labeling thoughts as good or bad.

Morning Practice

Current State:
Physical energy: _____
Emotional weather: _____
Mental clarity: _____

Awareness Intention: "Today I observe my thoughts like clouds passing in the sky."

What needs attention today?
_____
_____
_____

Three Gratitudes:
1. _____
2. _____
3. _____

Awareness Exploration

The loudest voice in my head says:
_____
_____
_____

When I make a mistake, I notice I:
_____
_____
_____

My mind tends to focus on:
- ☐ Past regrets
- ☐ Future worries
- ☐ Present moment
- ☐ Others' opinions

Evening Reflection

Today's Self-Talk Observations:
Critical moments: _____
_____

Neutral moments: _____
_____

Kind moments: _____
_____

Without Judgment, I Notice I:
_____
_____
_____

Small Victory:
_____
_____
_____

Surprising Discovery:
_____
_____
_____

Tracking Progress

Awareness Moments Today: _____ times

Most Common Thought Pattern:
- ☐ Comparison
- ☐ Perfectionism
- ☐ Worry
- ☐ Self-doubt
- ☐ Other: _____

Rate Your Day (1-10):
- Stayed neutral: _____
- Noticed patterns: _____
- Self-kindness: _____
- Present moment awareness: _____

Note for Tomorrow:
_____

Affirmation for Tonight:
"I am learning to observe myself with curiosity and compassion."

THE SPACE BETWEEN

Date: ____ / ____ / ____ • Day 33 of 90

Today's Theme: *Creating Space Between You and Your Thoughts*

You are not your thoughts. You're the awareness experiencing them.
Today, practice creating space.

Morning Practice

Right Now I Am:
Thinking: _____
Feeling: _____
Sensing: _____

The space between me and my thoughts feels:
- [ ] Nonexistent
- [ ] Tiny
- [ ] Growing
- [ ] Spacious

Today I'll Create Space By:
_____
_____

Three Gratitudes:
1. _____
2. _____
3. _____

Defending Awareness

When difficult thoughts arise, I can:
- [ ] Notice them
- [ ] Name them
- [ ] Let them pass
- [ ] Return to breath

I'm beginning to see that my thoughts are:
_____
_____

The story I tell myself most often:
_____
_____

Evening Reflection

Moments of Space Today:
_____
_____
_____

I Separated from My Thoughts When:
_____
_____
_____

This Felt:
_____
_____
_____

Pattern Becoming Clearer:
_____
_____
_____

Awareness Victories

Check what you did today:
- ☐ Noticed a thought without believing it
- ☐ Observed an emotion without drowning
- ☐ Created pause before reacting
- ☐ Recognized a pattern
- ☐ Stayed present for 1 full minute

Insight Emerging:
_____
_____

Daily Tracking

Rate your experience (1-10):
- Mental spaciousness: _____
- Observer perspective: _____
- Reactivity level: _____
- Peace with thoughts: _____

Growing Edge:
_____
_____

Affirmation for Tonight:
"I am the awareness behind my thoughts, vast and unchanging."

PATTERNS AND THEMES ───────────────

Date: ____ / ____ / ____ • Day 34 of 90

Today's Theme: *Recognizing Recurring Patterns*

After three days of observation, patterns emerge.
Today, gently map your mental landscape.

Morning Practice

Midweek Check-in:
Energy level: _____ /10
Motivation: _____ /10
Resistance: _____ /10
Hope: _____ /10

Patterns I'm Noticing:
Morning thoughts tend to be: _____
Afternoon thoughts tend to be: _____
Evening thoughts tend to be: _____

Today's Focus: "I observe my patterns with compassion, knowing awareness is the first step to freedom."

Three Gratitudes:
1. _____
2. _____
3. _____

Pattern Mapping

My Mind's Favorite Topics:
1. _____
2. _____
3. _____

Triggers I've Identified:
☐ Morning routine
☐ Work situations
☐ Relationships
☐ Body image
☐ Past memories
☐ Future concerns

My Pattern Cycle Goes:
Trigger → _____ → _____ → Result

Evening Reflection

Today's Pattern Observations:
_____
_____

I Notice My Mind:
Returns to: _____
Avoids: _____
Seeks: _____

Breakthrough Moment:
_____
_____

What Patterns Serve Me:
_____
_____

What Patterns Don't:
_____
_____

Weekly Progress

Days completed: 34/90
Consistency rating: _____ /10
Key pattern identified: _____

Self-Appreciation:
_____
_____
_____

Daily Tracking

Rate today (1-10):
- Pattern recognition: _____
- Self-understanding: _____
- Compassion for patterns: _____
- Motivation to continue: _____

Weekend Intention:
_____

Affirmation for Tonight:
"My patterns developed for good reasons. I can update them with love.

THOUGHTS VS. FACTS

Date: ____/____/____ • Day 35 of 90

Today's Theme: *Distinguishing Thoughts from Reality*

Not everything you think is true. Today, practice separating thoughts from facts.

Morning Practice

Current Reality Check:
What's actually happening right now: _____

What my mind is adding: _____

Today I'll Practice Asking: "Is this thought true, or is it just a thought?"

Three Facts I Know:
1. I am here: _____
2. I am breathing: _____
3. I am willing: _____

Three Gratitudes:
1. _____
2. _____
3. _____

Thought Investigation

Common Thought: "I'm not good enough"
- Is this fact or opinion?: _____
- Evidence for: _____
- Evidence against: _____
- More accurate statement: _____

Another Frequent Thought:
- Fact or story? _____
- What's actually true: _____

Evening Reflection

Thoughts I Questioned Today:
1. _____
   Verdict: _____
2. _____
   Verdict: _____

Surprising Discovery:
_____
_____
_____

When I Examined Evidence:
- When I realized: _____
- I felt: _____
- I could then: _____

Evidence Patterns

My Critic Tends To:
- ☐ Ignore positive evidence
- ☐ Magnify negative evidence
- ☐ Create false evidence
- ☐ Generalize from one instance
- ☐ Assume without checking

One False Belief to Release:
_____
_____
_____

Daily Tracking

Rate your experience (1-10):
- Critical thoughts examined: _____
- Found to be false/distorted: _____
- Successfully reframed: _____
- Truth clarity (1-10): _____

Legal Precedent Set:
"My thoughts are not always facts. I can investigate."

THE WITNESS WITHIN ───────────────

Date: ____ / ____ / ____ • Day 36 of 90

Today's Theme: *Strengthening Your Inner Observer*

You've been practicing all week.
Today, consciously strengthen the part of you that watches without judgment.

Morning Practice

The Witness Awakens:
Right now, I can observe: _____
Without becoming: _____
This observing self feels: _____

My Witness is Getting Stronger When:
_____
_____

Today I'll Practice Asking: "I am the calm awareness observing the storm of thoughts."

Three Gratitudes:
1. _____
2. _____
3. _____

Witness Development

From My Observer Perspective:
My patterns look like: _____
My growth looks like: _____
My resistance looks like: _____

The Witness Notices Without:
- ☐ Judging
- ☐ Fixing
- ☐ Analyzing
- ☐ Criticizing
- ☐ Attaching

What My Witness Sees Clearly
_____
_____
_____

Evening Reflection

Witness Moments Today:
_____
_____
_____

I Stayed in Observer Mode When:
_____
_____
_____

This Allowed Me To:
_____
_____
_____

The Witness Within Me Is:
- ☐ Awakening
- ☐ Strengthening
- ☐ Steadying
- ☐ Expanding

Week Closing In

6 Days of Awareness Have Shown Me:
_____
_____
_____

My Relationship with My Thoughts:
Before this week: _____
Now: _____

Daily Tracking

Rate your witness strength (1-10):
- Observer clarity: _____
- Non-attachment: _____
- Inner calm: _____
- Perspective gained: _____

Tomorrow's Completion Intention:
_____
_____

Affirmation for Tonight:
"The witness within me grows stronger and more peaceful each day."

WEEK 1 INTEGRATION

Date: ___/___/___ • Day 37 of 90

Today's Theme: *Celebrating Awareness*
You've completed your first week! Today, integrate what you've learned.

Morning Practice

Week 1 Reflection:
I started this week feeling: _____
I'm ending it feeling: _____

Awareness Victories This Week:
- ☐ Noticed patterns
- ☐ Created space
- ☐ Questioned thoughts
- ☐ Stayed neutral
- ☐ Strengthened witness
- ☐ Showed up daily

Three Deep Gratitudes:
1. _____
2. _____
3. _____

Week 1 Harvest

Key Patterns Discovered:
1. _____
2. _____
3. _____

Biggest Insight: _____
What Surprised Me: _____
What I'm Ready to Release: _____
What I Want to Strengthen: _____

Evening Celebration

I Completed Week 1!
Rating the week (1-10):
• Consistency: ___ • Growth: ___ • Self-compassion: ___ • Awareness gained: ___

Three Things I'm Proud Of:
1. _____
2. _____
3. _____

How I've Changed in 7 Days: _____
My Commitment for Week 2: _____

Weekly Tracking Summary

Average daily ratings:
• Self-compassion: ___ • Inner critic: ___ • Awareness: ___ • Wellbeing: ___

Note to Future Self: _____

Week 1 Affirmation: "I have successfully built the foundation of awareness. I am ready for Week 2."
Celebration Activity: How will you honor this milestone? _____

Continue to Week 2 ⟶

Building on Awareness

Challenging Critical Thoughts

Days 31-37 of Your Practice

This week's focus: Learning to question and reframe the critical thoughts you noticed in Week 1.

Last week you built awareness. You noticed patterns, created space, and strengthened your inner observer. Now you're ready to actively work with critical thoughts—not by fighting them, but by examining them with curiosity and responding with wisdom.

Week 2 Intentions

- Question the validity of critical thoughts
- Identify cognitive distortions
- Practice thought replacement
- Develop helpful responses
- Build your reframe toolkit

Daily Structure This Week

We're not trying to eliminate all negative thoughts—that's impossible. Instead, we're learning to:

1. Catch critical thoughts quickly
2. Examine them objectively
3. Respond helpfully
4. Choose what to believe

Your Week 2 Mantra

"I can question my thoughts. I can choose my response. I can rewrite my inner dialogue."

CATCHING THE CRITIC ─────────────────────────

Date: ____/____/____ • Day 38 of 90

Today's Theme: *Quick Recognition*
The faster you catch critical thoughts, the less power they have. Today, practice immediate recognition.

Morning Practice

Week 2 Energy Check:
Physical: _____ /10
Mental: _____ /10
Emotional: _____ /10
Motivation: _____ /10

Today's Intention: "I catch critical thoughts quickly and respond with curiosity."

Three Morning Gratitudes:
1. _____
2. _____
3. _____

Critic Catching Practice

My Critic's Favorite Phrases:
1. "You always _____"
2. "You never _____"
3. "You should _____"
4. "Why can't you _____"

Early Warning Signs the Critic is Active:
Body: _____
Emotions: _____
Energy: _____

Today I'll Catch My Critic By:
☐ Setting hourly check-ins
☐ Noting body tension
☐ Tracking mood shifts
☐ Other: _____

Evening Reflection

Critical Thoughts Caught Today:
Morning: _____

Afternoon: _____

Evening: _____

Speed of Recognition:
☐ Immediate
☐ Within minutes
☐ Within an hour
☐ After the fact

When I Caught the Critic Quickly:
What happened: _____

How I responded: _____

The outcome: _____

Tracking Progress

Critic Catches Today: _____ times

Most Effective Catching Method:
_____
_____

Pattern Noticed:
The critic is loudest when: _____

Daily Ratings

Rate your day (1-10):
- Critic awareness: _____
- Self-compassion: _____
- Overall progress: _____

Tomorrow's Focus:
_____
_____

Evening Affirmation:
"I'm getting faster at recognizing critical thoughts. Awareness is power."

THE EVIDENCE TEST

Date: ___ /___ /___ • Day 39 of 90

Today's Theme: *Examining the Evidence*
Critical thoughts feel true but often aren't. Today, put them on trial.

Morning Practice

Present State:
I woke up thinking: _____
Evidence this is true: _____
Evidence against: _____

Court is in Session: "Today I examine evidence before believing my thoughts."

Three Gratitudes for My Journey:
1. _____
2. _____
3. _____

The Evidence Test

Critical Thought #1: _____
Evidence FOR this thought:
- _____
- _____

Evidence AGAINST:
- _____
- _____
- _____

Verdict:
☐ True   ☐ Partially true   ☐ False   ☐ Distorted

More Accurate Statement:
_____

Critical Thought #2: _____
Evidence review:
- Supporting facts: _____
- Contradicting facts: _____

Reality Check:
What would a friend say? _____

Evening Reflection

Thoughts I Put on Trial:
1. _____
    Verdict: _____
2. _____
    Verdict: _____

Surprising Discovery:
_____
_____
_____

When I Examined Evidence:
- When I realized: _____
- I felt: _____
- I could then: _____

Evidence Patterns

My Critic Tends To:
- ☐ Ignore positive evidence
- ☐ Magnify negative evidence
- ☐ Create false evidence
- ☐ Generalize from one instance
- ☐ Assume without checking

One False Belief to Release:
_____
_____
_____

Daily Tracking

- Critical thoughts examined: _____
- Found to be false/distorted: _____
- Successfully reframed: _____
- Truth clarity (1–10): _____

Legal Precedent Set:
"My thoughts are not always facts. I can investigate."

NAMING DISTORTIONS

Date: ___/___/___ • Day 40 of 90

Today's Theme: *Identifying Thinking Errors*

When you name a distortion, you reduce its power.
Today, become familiar with your mind's favorite tricks.

Morning Practice

Distortion Check-in:
First thought today: _____
Type of distortion: _____
Reframe: _____

Today's Mission: "I recognize and name thought distortions as they arise."

Three Gratitudes:
1. _____
2. _____
3. _____

Distortion Dictionary

Check Your Top 3 Patterns:

- [ ] **All-or-Nothing**
  "If I'm not perfect, I'm a failure"

- [ ] **Mind Reading**
  "They think I'm incompetent"

- [ ] **Fortune Telling**
  "This will definitely go badly"

- [ ] **Magnification**
  "This mistake ruins everything"

- [ ] **Minimization**
  "My success doesn't count"

- [ ] **Personalization**
  "It's all my fault"

- [ ] **Should Statements**
  "I should be further along"

- [ ] **Emotional Reasoning**
  "I feel stupid, so I must be"

My #1 Distortion: _____
How It Shows Up: _____

Evening Reflection

Distortions Named Today:

Time	Thought	Distortion Type	Reframe
Morning	_____	_____	_____
Afternoon	_____	_____	_____
Evening	_____	_____	_____

Naming Distortions Helped Me:
_____
_____
_____

Pattern Recognition:
My mind loves to use: _____
Especially when: _____

Distortion Antidotes

For All-or-Nothing: Look for the middle ground
For Mind Reading: Check assumptions
For Fortune Telling: Stay present
For Magnification: Right-size it
For Personalization: Share responsibility

My Most Helpful Antidote:
_____
_____

Daily Tracking

- Distortions identified: _____
- Successfully reframed: _____
- Caught before believing: _____
- Mental flexibility (1-10): _____

Affirmation:
"I can see through my mind's distortions to the truth beneath."

THE REFRAME PRACTICE

Date: ____/____/____ • Day 41 of 90

Today's Theme: *Creating Helpful Alternatives*

For every critical thought, there's a kinder, truer alternative. Today, master the reframe.

Morning Practice

Reframe Warm-up:
"I'm terrible at this" becomes: _____
"I always fail" becomes: _____
"I'm not enough" becomes: _____

Today's Practice: "I transform critical thoughts into supportive truths."

Three Things I'm Learning:
1. _____
2. _____
3. _____

Reframe Workshop

Critical Thought: _____

Step 1: Acknowledge
"I notice I'm thinking _____"

Step 2: Validate
"It makes sense because _____"

Step 3: Question
"Is this helpful? _____ Is it true? _____"

Step 4: Reframe
"A more helpful thought: _____"

Step 5: Evidence
"This is true because _____"

Practice Round 2:
Critical: _____
Reframe: _____
Evidence: _____

Evening Reflection

Today's Best Reframes:
1. From: _____
   To: _____
2. From: _____
   To: _____

Reframing Felt:
Easy when: _____
Hard when: _____

Breakthrough Moment:
_____
_____
_____

Reframe Library

Building My Personal Collection:
For "I'm not good enough":
→ _____
For "I should be further along":
→ _____
For "Everyone else has it together":
→ _____
For my specific pattern:
→ _____

Daily Tracking

- Thoughts reframed: _____
- Reframes that stuck: _____
- Mood improvement: _____
- Hope level (1-10): _____

Power Statement
_____
_____
_____

Affirmation:
"I have the power to reframe any thought into something helpful."

THE FRIEND PERSPECTIVE ───────────────────────

Date: ____ / ____ / ____ • Day 42 of 90

Today's Theme: *What Would You Tell a Friend?*
You'd never speak to a friend the way your critic speaks to you. Today, access your inner wise friend.

Morning Practice

Friend Check:
If my best friend had my exact situation, I'd tell them: _____

So I Tell Myself: _____

Today's Commitment: "I speak to myself as I would to someone I love."

Three Appreciations:
1. I appreciate my: _____
2. I appreciate how I: _____
3. I appreciate that I: _____

The Friend Filter

Situation: _____
What My Critic Says: _____

What I'd Tell a Friend: _____

The Difference:
Tone: _____
Content: _____
Compassion level: _____

Applying Friend Wisdom to Myself:
_____
_____
_____

Evening Reflection

Friend Voice Moments:
I used my friend voice when: _____
It helped me: _____

I forgot and used critic voice when: _____
Next time I'll: _____

The Friend Within Me Says:
About today: _____
About my progress: _____
About tomorrow: _____

Building The Friend Voice

My Inner Friend's Qualities:
- [ ] Patient
- [ ] Encouraging
- [ ] Honest but kind
- [ ] Supportive
- [ ] Believing in me
- [ ] Other: _____

One Thing My Friend Voice Wants Me to Know:
_____
_____
_____

Daily Tracking

- Used friend voice: _____ times
- Caught critic voice: _____ times
- Self-compassion (1-10): _____
- Inner support (1-10): _____

Friend Voice Affirmation:
"I have access to an inner friend who loves and supports me always."

BUILDING NEW PATHWAYS ─────────────

Date: ____ / ____ / ____ • Day 43 of 90

Today's Theme: *Repetition Creates New Patterns*
You're not just challenging old thoughts; you're building new neural pathways. Today, strengthen the new.

Morning Practice

Neural Pathway Check:
Old pathway says: _____
New pathway says: _____
Today I'll practice: _____

Repetition Commitment: "Each kind thought creates a stronger pathway to self-love."

Three Wins This Week:
1. _____
2. _____
3. _____

Pathway Strengthening

New Thought to Practice: _____

Repetition Schedule:
- ☐ Morning: Said it ✓
- ☐ Midday: Said it ✓
- ☐ Afternoon: Said it ✓
- ☐ Evening: Said it ✓

Each Time It Feels:
1st time: _____
2nd time: _____
3rd time: _____
4th time: _____

Evidence This New Thought Is True:
1. _____
2. _____
3. _____

Evening Reflection

Pathway Progress:

Old thought frequency: Decreased / Same / Increased

New thought frequency: Increased / Same / Decreased

The New Pathway Feels:
- ☐ Foreign
- ☐ Awkward
- ☐ Possible
- ☐ Growing
- ☐ Natural

Today's Repetitions:
Morning thought: _____ times
Caught and switched: _____ times
Felt believable: _____ times

Neuroplasticity In Action

I'm Rewiring My Brain By:
_____
_____
_____

Old Pattern Weakening:
I notice: _____
_____

New Pattern Strengthening:
I notice: _____
_____

Tracking Transformation

- New thought repetitions: _____
- Felt natural (1-10): _____
- Old thought intensity (1-10): _____
- Brain flexibility (1-10): _____

Tomorrow's Practice:
_____
_____

Neuroplasticity Affirmation:
"I have access to an inner friend who loves and supports me always."

WEEK 2 INTEGRATION ─────────────────────────

Date: ____ / ____ / ____ • Day 44 of 90

Today's Theme: *Celebrating Your Challenger Spirit*

Two weeks complete! You've built awareness AND learned to challenge critical thoughts.

Morning Practice

Two-Week Reflection:
I started this week feeling: _____
I'm ending it feeling: _____

Today's Celebration Intention: "I honor my progress and my courage to challenge old patterns."

Gratitude for My Growth:
1. _____
2. _____
3. _____

Week 2 Harvest

Critical Thought Tools Gained:
- ☐ Quick recognition ☐ Distortion naming ☐ Friend perspective
- ☐ Evidence testing ☐ Reframe practice ☐ New pathways

Biggest Breakthrough: _____

Most Powerful Reframe:
From: _____
To: _____

What's Different Now:
My inner dialogue has shifted from: _____
To: _____

Evening Integration

Days completed: 44/90   Growth felt: ____ /10
Consistency: ____ /10   Confidence building: ____ /10

Three Proud Moments:
1. _____
2. _____
3. _____

My Critic Has:
☐ Gotten quieter ☐ Less believable ☐ More recognizable ☐ Less powerful

I Have:
☐ More awareness ☐ More tools ☐ More hope ☐ More self-compassion

Week 2 Summary

Average daily ratings:
- Critic awareness: ____ • Reframe success: ____ • Self-compassion: ____
- Mental flexibility: ____

A Letter to Week 3 Me: _____

Integration Affirmation: "I have successfully learned to challenge critical thoughts. I'm ready for body compassion."

Celebration: How will you honor these two weeks? _____

Continue to Week 3 ⟶

Healing Your Relationship with Your Physical Self

Body Compassion
Days 45-51 of Your Practice

This week's focus: Developing kindness and appreciation for your body, regardless of its shape, size, or condition.

Your body has carried you through every moment of your life. It's been the vessel for all your experiences, yet it often receives the harshest criticism. This week, you'll practice relating to your body with gratitude, respect, and compassion.

Week 3 Intentions

- Notice body-critical thoughts without judgment
- Practice body gratitude and appreciation
- Develop body-neutral language
- Honor your body's needs and signals
- Build a compassionate body relationship

Important Note

Body compassion isn't about loving every aspect of your appearance. It's about:

- Respecting what your body does for you
- Treating it with care
- Speaking to it kindly
- Accepting it as it is today
- Honoring its wisdom

This Week's Approach

"My body deserves kindness simply for keeping me alive."

BODY AWARENESS

Date: ____/____/____ • Day 45 of 90

Today's Theme: *Noticing Without Judging*
Before we can change our relationship with our body, we need awareness of how we currently relate to it.

Morning Practice

Body Check-in:
Head: _____
Shoulders/neck: _____
Chest/heart: _____
Stomach: _____
Back: _____
Legs/feet: _____

Without Judgment, My Body Feels:
_____
_____

Today's Intention: "I notice my body with curiosity and neutrality."

Three Gratitudes for My Body:
1. _____
2. _____
3. _____

Body Awareness Exploration

How I Currently Speak to My Body:
Morning mirror: _____
During movement: _____
When tired: _____
When in pain: _____

My Body Criticism Patterns:
- ☐ Appearance focus
- ☐ Comparison to others
- ☐ Comparison to past self
- ☐ Performance demands
- ☐ Ignoring its needs

One Thing My Body Did for Me Today:
_____
_____

Evening Reflection

Body Awareness Moments:
I noticed criticism when: _____
_____

I noticed appreciation when: _____
_____

I noticed neutrality when: _____
_____

My Body Carried Me Through:
_____
_____
_____

Without My Body, I Couldn't Have:
_____
_____
_____

Neuroplasticity In Action

Current Relationship with Body:
- ☐ Hostile
- ☐ Critical
- ☐ Disconnected
- ☐ Neutral
- ☐ Accepting
- ☐ Appreciative

One Shift I Want to Make:
_____
_____

Daily Tracking

- Body-critical thoughts: _____
- Body-neutral thoughts: _____
- Body-appreciative thoughts: _____
- Body connection (1-10): _____

Body Wisdom Noticed:
_____
_____

Affirmation:
"My body is worthy of respect and kindness, exactly as it is today."

Body Scan Meditation Practice

5-Minute Body Scan Instructions

Find a comfortable position. Close your eyes or soften your gaze.

Starting at Your Head:
- Notice sensations in your scalp, forehead, eyes
- No need to change anything, just notice
- "Hello, head. Thank you for thinking and dreaming"

Moving to Face and Neck:
- Awareness of jaw, cheeks, throat
- Often holds tension – just acknowledge
- "Hello, face. Thank you for expressing"

Shoulders and Arms:
- Feel the weight, temperature, any sensation
- Notice without judgment
- "Hello, arms. Thank you for holding and creating"

Chest and Heart:
- Notice breath moving in and out
- Feel heartbeat if possible
- "Hello, heart. Thank you for feeling and pumping life"

Belly and Back:
- Soft attention to core
- Notice support of spine
- "Hello, center. Thank you for digesting and supporting"

Hips and Pelvis:
- Often ignored area – bring gentle awareness
- "Hello, foundation. Thank you for stability"

Legs and Feet:
- Feel connection to ground
- Notice strength and tiredness
- "Hello, legs. Thank you for carrying me"

Whole Body Awareness:
- Sense your body as complete
- One interconnected system
- "Hello, body. Thank you for everything"

BODY GRATITUDE

Date: ____ / ____ / ____ • Day 46 of 90

Today's Theme: *Appreciating Function Over Form*
Your body is a miracle of function. Today, focus on what it does, not how it looks.

Morning Practice

Gratitude for Function:
My eyes let me: _____
My hands let me: _____
My legs let me: _____
My heart keeps me: _____

Function-Focused Intention: "Today I appreciate my body for what it does, not how it appears."

Three Body Miracles:
1. _____
2. _____
3. _____

Body Appreciation Practice

Systems Working for Me Right Now:
- ☐ Heart pumping blood
- ☐ Lungs breathing automatically
- ☐ Digestive system processing
- ☐ Immune system protecting
- ☐ Nervous system communicating
- ☐ Muscles holding me up

My Body Has Survived:
_____
_____

My Body Has Healed From:
_____
_____

My Body Allows Me To:
Connect with: _____
Experience: _____
Create: _____
Enjoy: _____

Evening Reflection

Body Gratitude Moments:
This morning my body: _____
This afternoon my body: _____
This evening my body: _____

Function I Usually Take for Granted:
_____
_____
_____

When I Focus on Function:
I feel: _____
I notice: _____
I appreciate: _____

Shifting Perspective

Instead of Criticizing: _____
_____

I Can Appreciate: _____
_____

My Body's Resilience:
It continues to: _____
Despite: _____

Daily Tracking

- Function appreciations: _____
- Appearance criticisms: _____
- Gratitude moments: _____
- Body respect (1-10): _____

One Function to Celebrate:
_____
_____
_____

Gratitude Affirmation:
"I am grateful for all the ways my body supports my life."

Body Appreciation Exercises

The Function Letter

Write a thank-you letter to a body part you usually criticize, focusing only on what it does:

"Dear [body part],

Thank you for [specific functions].

Because of you, I can [activities]. You've carried me through [experiences].

You deserve respect for [specific work you do]."

The Timeline Appreciation

- Age 5: My body learned to _____
- Age 10: My body could _____
- Age 15: My body survived _____
- Age 20: My body accomplished _____
- Today: My body continues to _____

The Daily Miracle List

Count the miraculous things your body did today without your conscious effort:

- Heartbeats (about 100,000)
- Breaths (about 20,000)
- Steps taken: _____
- Cells renewed (millions)
- Toxins filtered
- Food digested
- Temperature regulated

BODY NEUTRALITY ───────────────────────

Date: ____ / ____ / ____ • Day 47 of 90

Today's Theme: *Finding the Middle Ground*
You don't have to love your body's appearance. Neutrality is enough. Today, practice body-neutral language.

Morning Practice

Neutral Observations:
My body is: (factual, not judgmental)
_____
_____

Neutral Language Practice:
Instead of "fat/skinny" → "My body is a body"
Instead of "ugly/beautiful" → "This is how I look"
Instead of "good/bad" → "This is neutral"

Today's Neutral Intention: "My body doesn't need to be beautiful to be valuable."

Three Neutral Facts:
1. I have a body: _____
2. It exists in space: _____
3. It functions: _____

Body Neutral Language

Rewriting Critical Statements:
Critical: "I hate my _____"
Neutral: "I have a _____"

Critical: "My _____ is too _____"
Neutral: "My _____ is _____"

Critical: "I need to fix my _____"
Neutral: "My _____ exists as it is"

Body Parts I Can Be Neutral About:
_____
_____
_____

Evening Reflection

Neutral Language Practice:
Times I used neutral language: _____
Times I slipped into judgment: _____
Times I caught and corrected: _____

Neutrality Felt:
- ☐ Strange
- ☐ Relief
- ☐ Peaceful
- ☐ Boring
- ☐ Free

Discoveries About Neutrality:
_____
_____
_____

The Neutral Zone

One Shift I Want to Make:
_____
_____
_____

What Judgment Takes Away:
_____
_____
_____

Body Parts Easier to Be Neutral About:
_____
_____
_____

Parts Needing More Practice:
_____
_____
_____

Daily Tracking

- Neutral statements: _____
- Judgmental statements: _____
- Corrections made: _____
- Peace level (1-10): _____

Neutral Truth:
"My body is a body. It doesn't need to earn its right to exist."

Neutral Language Examples

Instead of Judgment → Use Neutral Facts:

Body Part Descriptions:
- "Fat arms" → "Arms"
- "Skinny legs" → "Legs"
- "Ugly scar" → "Scar from [year/event]"
- "Huge thighs" → "Thighs"
- "Flabby stomach" → "Stomach" or "Soft belly"

Physical Descriptions:
- "I look terrible" → "This is how I look today"
- "I'm disgusting" → "I have a human body"
- "I'm too heavy/thin" → "My body has this shape"
- "I'm getting old and saggy" → "My body is aging"

Ability Descriptions:
- "I'm so out of shape" → "My current fitness level"
- "I'm weak" → "Building strength"
- "I can't do anything" → "I can do [specific things]"
- "My body is failing" → "My body is adjusting"

Neutral Response Scripts

When others comment on appearance:
- "Thanks for noticing me" (instead of agreeing/disagreeing)
- "Bodies come in all shapes" (educational redirect)
- "I'm focusing on how I feel" (boundary setting)
- "That's one perspective" (neutral acknowledgment)

When comparing to others:
- "Every body is different"
- "They have their body, I have mine"
- "Comparison isn't useful for me"
- "I'm on my own journey"

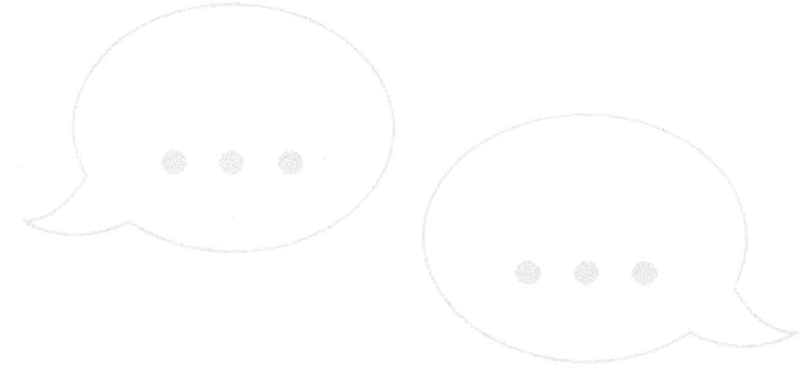

BODY KINDNESS

Date: ____/____/____ • Day 48 of 90

Today's Theme: *Speaking to Your Body Like a Friend*

Your body responds to how you speak to it. Today, practice kindness.

Morning Practice

Body Wisdom Check
- ☐ Heart pumping blood
- ☐ Lungs breathing automatically
- ☐ Digestive system processing
- ☐ Immune system protecting
- ☐ Nervous system communicating
- ☐ Muscles holding me up

Today's Kindness Commitment: "I speak to my body with the same kindness I'd show a dear friend."

Three Kind Truths:

1. My body tries its best: _____

2. My body deserves: _____

3. My body needs: _____

Body Kindness Practice

Kind Responses to Body Signals:
When tired: "Thank you for signaling. Let's rest."
When hungry: _____
When sore: _____
When energized: _____
When uncomfortable: _____

Apologies My Body Deserves:
"I'm sorry for: _____"
"I'm sorry I said: _____"
"I'm sorry I ignored: _____"

Promises to My Body:
_____
_____
_____

Evening Reflection

Kind Words Spoken to Body:
_____
_____
_____

My Body Responded to Kindness By:
_____
_____
_____

Harsh Words I Caught and Changed:
From: _____
_____
To: _____
_____

Building Body Kindness

Kind Things to Say Daily:
Morning: _____
During meals: _____
During movement: _____
Before sleep: _____

My Body Deserves Kindness Because:
_____
_____
_____

Daily Tracking

- Kind body statements: _____
- Critical statements caught: _____
- Body response noticed: _____
- Self-compassion (1-10): _____

One Function to Celebrate:
_____
_____
_____

Kindness Affirmation:
"My body deserves gentle words and loving care."

BODY WISDOM

Date: ___ / ___ / ___ • Day 49 of 90

Today's Theme: *Listening to Your Body's Intelligence*

Your body has wisdom. It knows what it needs. Today, practice listening.

Morning Practice

Body Wisdom Check:
My body is telling me it needs:
- ☐ Rest
- ☐ Movement
- ☐ Nourishment
- ☐ Touch
- ☐ Breath
- ☐ Release

Honoring the Message:
Today I will listen by: _____

Wisdom Intention: "My body knows. I trust its signals and honor its needs."

Three Times My Body Was Right:
1. _____
2. _____
3. _____

Listening Practice

Body Signals and Meanings:
Tension in shoulders = _____
Knot in stomach = _____
Heaviness in chest = _____
Energy surge = _____
Fatigue = _____

My Body's Yes Feels Like:
_____
_____

My Body's No Feels Like:
_____
_____

Wisdom I've Been Ignoring:
_____
_____

Evening Reflection

Body Wisdom Moments:
I listened when: _____
Result: _____
I ignored when: _____
Result: _____

My Body Knew:
_____
_____
_____

Trusting Body Wisdom

Signals I'm Learning to Trust:
_____
_____
_____

My Body is Teaching Me:
_____
_____
_____

Tomorrow I Will Honor:
_____
_____
_____

Daily Tracking

- Body signals noticed: _____
- Signals honored: _____
- Wisdom followed: _____
- Body trust (1-10): _____

Wisdom Recognition:
"My body holds intelligence. I'm learning to listen."

BODY CARE ─────────────────────────────

Date: ____/____/____ • Day 50 of 90

Today's Theme: *Caring Actions as Love Language*

Show your body love through caring actions, not just words.

Morning Practice

Care Inventory:
- Sleep last night: _____ hours
- Water yesterday: _____ glasses
- Nourishment: Adequate/Insufficient
- Movement: Gentle/Intense/None
- Rest: Enough/Not enough

Care Intention: "Today I show my body love through concrete caring actions."

Three Caring Actions for Today:

1. _____
2. _____
3. _____

Body Care Practice

Small Acts of Care:
- ☐ Drink water mindfully
- ☐ Eat without distraction
- ☐ Take stretching breaks
- ☐ Rest when tired
- ☐ Move joyfully
- ☐ Breathe deeply
- ☐ Touch gently

One Special Treat for My Body:
_____
_____

My Body's Current Needs:
Physical: _____
Emotional: _____
Sensory: _____

Care I Will Provide:
_____
_____

Evening Reflection

Care Provided Today:
Morning: _____
Afternoon: _____
Evening: _____

My Body's Response to Care:
_____
_____
_____

Care That Felt Best:
_____
_____
_____

Sustainable Body Care

Daily Non-Negotiables:
1. _____
2. _____
3. _____

Weekly Body Care:
_____
_____
_____

When My Body is Cared For:
I feel: _____
I can: _____

Daily Tracking

- Caring actions taken: _____
- Body's response: _____
- Energy level: _____
- Overall wellbeing (1-10): _____

Care Affirmation:
"Caring for my body is an act of self-love."

WEEK 3 INTEGRATION

Date: ____ / ____ / ____ • Day 51 of 90

Today's Theme: *Celebrating Body Compassion*

Three weeks complete! You've transformed criticism into awareness, challenged thoughts, and now built body compassion.

Morning Practice

Three-Week Reflection:
Week 1: Built awareness   Week 2: Challenged thoughts
Week 3: Embraced body compassion
Together: _____

Celebration Intention: "I honor my growing compassion for my body and myself."

Body Appreciation:
1. Thank you for: _____
2. I appreciate: _____
3. I'm learning: _____

Week 3 Harvest

Body Compassion Tools:
☐ Awareness without judgment   ☐ Neutral language   ☐ Listening to wisdom
☐ Gratitude for function   ☐ Kind communication   ☐ Caring actions

Biggest Body Shift:
From: _____
To: _____

My Body and I:
Beginning of week: _____
End of week: _____

Evening Integration

Days completed: 51/90   Overall self-compassion (1-10): ____
Body relationship (1-10): ____   Motivation to continue (1-10): ____

Three Body Victories:
1. _____
2. _____
3. _____

Changes I Notice:
- How I see my body: _____
- How I speak to it: _____
- How I care for it: _____

Week 3 Summary

Average daily ratings:
• Body criticism (lower is better): ____   • Body compassion: ____
• Body connection: ____   • Mental flexibility: ____

Message to My Body: _____

Three-Week Affirmation: "I have spent 51 days building awareness, challenging criticism, and embracing my body with compassion. I am transforming."

Celebration: How will you honor three weeks of practice? _____

Continue to Week 4 ⟶

Welcoming All Feelings Without Judgment

Emotional Acceptance

Days 52–58 of Your Practice

This week's focus: Learning to accept and validate all emotions as valid messengers, not problems to fix.

You've built awareness, challenged critical thoughts, and developed body compassion. Now you'll extend that same acceptance to your emotional world. Every emotion—even the uncomfortable ones—has value and wisdom to offer.

Week 4 Intentions

- Notice emotions without immediately trying to change them
- Validate feelings as legitimate responses
- Understand emotions as messengers
- Practice emotional tolerance
- Develop emotional wisdom

Reframing Emotions

This week, we shift from:

- I shouldn't feel this way" → "This feeling is telling me something"
- "This emotion is bad" → "This emotion is uncomfortable but valid"
- "I need to fix this" → "I need to feel this"
- "I'm too emotional" → "I'm human"

Your Week 4 Foundation

"All emotions are valid. They're data, not directives."

EMOTIONAL AWARENESS ───────────────────────

Date: ____ / ____ / ____ • Day 52 of 90

Today's Theme: *Naming and Noticing*

You can't accept what you don't acknowledge.
Today, build awareness of your emotional landscape.

Morning Practice

Emotional Weather Report:
Right now I feel: _____
Intensity (1-10): _____
Location in body: _____
Been present since: _____

Today's Emotional Intention: "I notice and name my emotions without judgment."

Three Gratitudes:
1. _____
2. _____
3. _____

Emotional Awareness Map

Emotions Present Today:
- ☐ Joy
- ☐ Shame
- ☐ Peace
- ☐ Love
- ☐ Sadness
- ☐ Guilt
- ☐ Frustration
- ☐ Loneliness
- ☐ Anger
- ☐ Excitement
- ☐ Hope
- ☐ Fear
- ☐ Anxiety
- ☐ Grief
- ☐ Other: _____

Primary Emotion: _____
Secondary Emotions: _____

I Tend to:
- ☐ Minimize emotions
- ☐ Amplify emotions
- ☐ Avoid emotions
- ☐ Analyze emotions
- ☐ Judge emotions

Evening Reflection

Emotional Journey Today:
Morning emotions: _____
Afternoon emotions: _____
Evening emotions: _____

Emotions I Welcomed:
_____
_____
_____

Emotions I Resisted:
_____
_____
_____

When I Simply Named Without Judging:
The emotion was: _____
I noticed: _____

Awareness Insights

Emotions I'm Comfortable With:
_____
_____

Emotions I Struggle With:
_____
_____

Pattern Noticed:
_____
_____

Daily Tracking

- Different emotions felt: _____
- Emotions named: _____
- Judgments noticed: _____
- Emotional awareness (1-10): _____

Discovery:
_____
_____

Affirmation:
"I can notice and name my emotions without becoming them."

EMOTIONAL VALIDATION ─────────────

Date: ____ / ____ / ____ • Day 53 of 90

Today's Theme: *Your Feelings Make Sense*
Every emotion has a reason. Today, practice validating your feelings.

Morning Practice

Validation Check:
I'm feeling: _____
This makes sense because: _____
Anyone in my situation might feel: _____

Validation Intention: "All my emotions are valid responses to my experiences."

Three Emotional Truths:
1. My feelings matter because: _____
2. I have a right to feel: _____
3. My emotions are: _____

Validation Practice

Current Feeling: _____

Validation Statements:
"Of course I feel _____ because _____"
"It makes complete sense that _____"
"Anyone would feel _____ if _____"
"This emotion is telling me _____"

Historical Validation:
This feeling connects to: _____
Past experience of: _____
Which explains why: _____

What This Emotion Needs:
- ☐ To be felt
- ☐ To be expressed
- ☐ To be witnessed
- ☐ To be honored
- ☐ Time to pass

Evening Reflection

Validation Moments:
I validated: _____
This helped me: _____
I invalidated: _____
Next time I'll: _____

The Power of Validation:
When I validate my feelings: _____
_____
When I invalidate them: _____
_____

Validation Breakthroughs

Emotion I Finally Validated:
_____
_____
_____

Why It Was Hard Before:
_____
_____
_____

What Changes When I Validate
_____
_____
_____

Daily Tracking

- Emotions validated: _____
- Self-judgments caught: _____
- Validation statements used: _____
- Emotional acceptance (1-10): _____

Validation Truth:
_____
_____
_____

Affirmation:
"My emotions are valid messengers deserving respect."

EMOTIONAL MESSAGES

Date: ____/____/____ • Day 54 of 90

Today's Theme: *Emotions as Wise Messengers*

Each emotion brings information. Today, listen to their messages.

Morning Practice

Message Check:
Current emotion: _____
Possible message: _____
What it might need: _____

Listening Intention: "I listen to my emotions' wisdom without shooting the messenger."

Three Things Emotions Have Taught Me:
1. _____
2. _____
3. _____

Emotional Wisdom Decoder

Common Messages:

Anger says: "A boundary was crossed"
My anger today says: _____

Sadness says: "Something needs to be grieved"
My sadness says: _____

Fear says: "Pay attention to safety"
My fear says: _____

Joy says: "More of this please"
My joy says: _____

Shame says: "I fear disconnection"
My shame says: _____

Message I've Been Missing:
_____
_____
_____

Evening Reflection

Messages Received Today:
Emotion: _____
Message: _____
Response: _____

Wisdom Gained:
_____
_____
_____

When I Listen to Emotions:
I learn: _____
I can: _____

Emotional Intelligence

Messages I'm Learning to Hear:
_____
_____
_____

Emotion I Misunderstood Before:
_____
_____
_____

Now I understand it means: _____

Tomorrow I'll Listen For:
_____
_____
_____

Daily Tracking

- Messages decoded: _____
- Wisdom gained: _____
- Actions taken from emotions: _____
- Emotional wisdom (1-10): _____

Key Message Today:
_____
_____

Affirmation:
"My emotions carry wisdom. I'm learning their language."

SITTING WITH FEELINGS

Date: ___/___/___ • Day 55 of 90

Today's Theme: *Emotional Tolerance*

Not all emotions need to be fixed. Some just need to be felt.
Today, practice sitting with feelings.

Morning Practice

Tolerance Check:
Emotion present: _____
Urge to: ☐ Fix ☐ Avoid ☐ Numb ☐ Distract
Instead I'll: ☐ Breathe ☐ Feel ☐ Allow ☐ Witness

Tolerance Intention: "I can feel emotions fully without being overwhelmed."

Three Times I Survived Big Emotions:

1. _____
2. _____
3. _____

Sitting Practice

Emotion to Sit With: _____

Set timer for 2 minutes:
Minute 1: Notice sensations: _____

Minute 2: Notice changes: _____

After Sitting:
The emotion: ☐ Intensified ☐ Softened ☐ Shifted ☐ Passed

What I Learned:
_____
_____

Comfort Strategies:
☐ Hand on heart
☐ Deep breathing
☐ Gentle movement
☐ Self-soothing words
☐ Grounding (5 senses)

Evening Reflection

Sitting Practice Results:
Emotions I sat with: _____
Duration tolerated: _____
What happened: _____
_____

Tolerance Building:
Morning tolerance: _____ /10
Evening tolerance: _____ /10

When I Don't Try to Fix:
The emotion: _____

Building Tolerance

Emotions Easier to Sit With:
_____
_____
_____

Emotions Still Challenging:
_____
_____
_____

My Tolerance is Growing:
Evidence: _____
_____
_____

Daily Tracking

- Emotions felt fully: _____
- Urges to fix resisted: _____
- Minutes of sitting: _____
- Tolerance level (1-10): _____

Tolerance Victory:
_____
_____
_____

Affirmation:
"I can feel my emotions fully and survive them all."

EMOTIONAL EXPRESSION ─────────────────

Date: ____/____/____ • Day 56 of 90

Today's Theme: *Healthy Expression*

Emotions need movement. Today, find healthy ways to express what you feel.

Morning Practice

Expression Check:
Emotion needing expression: _____
Current expression method: _____
Healthier option: _____

Expression Intention: "I express my emotions in ways that honor them and support me."

Three Healthy Expressions I've Used:

1. _____
2. _____
3. _____

Expression Toolkit

For Anger:
- ☐ Journal it out
- ☐ Physical movement
- ☐ Assertive communication
- ☐ Creative destruction (safely)

My way: _____

For Anxiety:
- ☐ List concerns
- ☐ Movement/shaking
- ☐ Breathing exercises
- ☐ Talk it through

My way: _____

For Sadness:
- ☐ Good cry
- ☐ Talk to someone
- ☐ Write a letter
- ☐ Create art

My way: _____

For Joy:
- ☐ Dance/movement
- ☐ Share with others
- ☐ Create something
- ☐ Celebrate

My way: _____

Evening Reflection

Expression Today:
Emotion expressed: _____
Method used: _____
How it felt: _____

Suppressed vs. Expressed:
When I suppress: _____
_____

When I express: _____
_____

Healthy Expression

New Expression Method Tried:
_____
_____
_____

Expression That Helped Most:
_____
_____
_____

Tomorrow's Expression Plan:
If I feel: _____
_____

I will: _____
_____

Daily Tracking

- Emotions expressed: _____
- Emotions suppressed: _____
- Expression methods used: _____
- Emotional freedom (1-10): _____

Expression Insight:
_____
_____
_____

Affirmation:
"I can express my emotions in ways that serve my wellbeing."

EMOTIONAL BALANCE

Date: ____/____/____ • Day 57 of 90

Today's Theme: *All Emotions in Proportion*

Balance isn't about being happy all the time.
It's about experiencing all emotions without getting stuck.

Morning Practice

Balance Check:
Dominant emotion lately: _____
Emotions I'm avoiding: _____
Emotions I'm ready to feel: _____

Balance Intention: "I allow all emotions their rightful place in my experience."

Three Signs of My Emotional Health:
1. _____
2. _____
3. _____

Balance Practice

Emotional Pie Chart:
Estimate percentage of time in each:
Joy: ____ %
Sadness: ____ %
Fear: ____ %
Anger: ____ %
Peace: ____ %
Other: ____ %

What's Missing:
_____
_____
_____

What's Dominating:
_____
_____
_____

Inviting Balance:
To balance _____ , I can invite more _____
By: _____

Evening Reflection

Today's Emotional Palette:
Morning: _____
Midday: _____
Evening: _____

Balance Noticed:
_____
_____

When Multiple Emotions Coexisted:
_____
_____

Finding Balance

Balance Looks Like:
_____
_____
_____

Balance Doesn't Mean:
_____
_____
_____

My Emotional Range is:
- ☐ Expanding
- ☐ Contracting
- ☐ Stabilizing
- ☐ Flowing

Daily Tracking

- Emotional variety: _____
- Stuck points: _____
- Flow moments: _____
- Balance level (1-10): _____

Balance Insight:
_____
_____

Affirmation:
"I can hold space for all emotions without losing myself."

WEEK 4 INTEGRATION ―――――――――――――――――――――

Date: ___ / ___ / ___ • Day 58 of 90

Today's Theme: *Celebrating Emotional Acceptance*

Four weeks! You've built awareness, challenged thoughts, embraced your body, and now accepted your emotions.

Morning Practice

Four-Week Journey:
Week 1: Awareness _____
Week 2: Challenging thoughts _____
Week 3: Body compassion _____
Week 4: Emotional acceptance _____

Integration Intention: "I celebrate my growing capacity to accept all parts of myself."

Emotional Gratitudes:
1. I'm grateful for my anger because: _____
2. I'm grateful for my sadness because: _____
3. I'm grateful for my fear because: _____

Week 4 Harvest

Emotional Tools Gained:
- ☐ Naming without judgment
- ☐ Validation practice
- ☐ Message decoding
- ☐ Sitting with feelings
- ☐ Healthy expression
- ☐ Emotional balance

Biggest Emotional Shift:
From: _____

To: _____

Emotion I've Made Peace With:
_____
_____
_____

Month 1 • Week 4: Emotional Acceptance

Evening Integration

58 Days of Practice:
Days completed: 58/90
Emotional growth (1-10): _____
Self-acceptance (1-10): _____
Inner peace (1-10): _____

Four-Week Victories:
1. _____
2. _____
3. _____
4. _____

I Now Understand:
About emotions: _____
About myself: _____
About healing: _____

Month 1 Closing

When Month 1 Started:
I was: _____
_____
_____

Now I am:
_____
_____
_____

Ready for Month 2 Because:
_____
_____
_____

Weekly Summary

Acceptance level: _____ /10
Acceptance level: _____ /10
Expression freedom: _____ /10
Overall growth: _____ /10

Month 1 Affirmation:
"I have spent 58 days building a foundation of self-awareness, self-challenge, self-compassion, and self-acceptance. I am transforming."

MONTH 1 COMPLETE

Date: ___/___/___ • Day 59-60 of 90

Day 59: Month Reflection

Morning Practice:
What I've learned about myself: _____
What I'm ready to release: _____
What I'm ready to receive: _____

Month 1 Key Insights:
1. _____
2. _____
3. _____

My Growing Edge:
_____
_____

Day 60: Integration & Rest

Morning Intention: "I honor my journey and prepare for continued growth."

Integration Questions:
How have I changed? _____
What patterns have shifted? _____
What still needs attention? _____

Month 1 Celebration:
Consistency: ___ /60 days
Growth felt: ___ /10
Ready for Month 2: ___ /10

How I'll Celebrate:
_____

Monthly Checkpoint

Safety & Wellbeing Check:
Energy level: ___ /10
Emotional stability: ___ /10
Support needed: Yes/No
If yes, I will: _____

Month 2 Intention:
_____

Message to Future Self:
_____
_____

Month 1 Complete!
You've built an incredible foundation. Rest, celebrate, and prepare for Month 2: Deepening Practice.

Continue to Month 2 ⟶

Month 2: Deepening Awareness

Boundaries & Needs
Days 61-67 of Your Practice

This week's focus: Learning to identify, communicate, and maintain healthy boundaries while recognizing and meeting your legitimate needs.

Month 1 built your foundation of awareness and acceptance. Now in Month 2, you'll deepen these practices by actively creating the conditions for self-love to flourish. Boundaries and needs are the architecture of self-respect.

Week 5 Intentions

- Identify where boundaries are needed
- Practice saying no with kindness
- Recognize legitimate needs vs. wants
- Communicate boundaries clearly
- Honor your needs without guilt

Understanding Boundaries

Boundaries aren't walls—they're guidelines that:

- Protect your energy
- Clarify expectations
- Prevent resentment
- Enable authentic connection
- Demonstrate self-respect

This Week's Foundation

"My boundaries protect my peace. My needs are valid and deserve attention."

BOUNDARY AWARENESS

Date: ____ / ____ / ____ • Day 61 of 90

Today's Theme: *Recognizing Where Boundaries Are Needed*
Before setting boundaries, notice where they're absent or violated.

Morning Practice

Month 2 Energy Check:
Physical reserves: ____ /10
Emotional capacity: ____ /10
Mental clarity: ____ /10
Motivation: ____ /10

Today's Intention: "I notice where boundaries are needed to protect my wellbeing."

Three Gratitudes: (This month: for your growth)
1. I'm grateful for my progress in: _____
2. I'm grateful for my ability to: _____
3. I'm grateful for learning: _____

Boundary Assessment

Where I Feel Drained:
- [ ] Work/career
- [ ] Family relationships
- [ ] Friendships
- [ ] Romantic relationship
- [ ] Social media
- [ ] Personal time
- [ ] Physical space

Signs My Boundaries Are Crossed:
Physical: _____
Emotional: _____
Mental: _____
Time/Energy: _____

One Boundary I Need:
_____
_____
_____

Evening Reflection

Boundary Awareness Today:
I noticed boundary crossing when: _____
My body's signal was: _____
I need protection from: _____

Without This Boundary:
I feel: _____
I lose: _____

With This Boundary:
I would feel: _____
I would gain: _____

Boundary Insights

Where I Give Too Much:
_____
_____
_____

Where I Accept Too Little:
_____
_____
_____

Pattern Recognized:
_____
_____
_____

Daily Tracking

- Boundary violations noticed: _____
- Energy level maintained: _____ /10
- Self-respect practiced: _____

Tomorrow's Focus:
_____
_____
_____

Affirmation:
"I deserve boundaries that protect my peace and energy."

IDENTIFYING YOUR NEEDS

Date: ___/___/___ • Day 62 of 90

Today's Theme: *Legitimate Needs vs. Wants*

Your needs matter. Today, identify what you genuinely need to thrive.

Morning Practice

Needs Check:
What I need physically: _____
What I need emotionally: _____
What I need mentally: _____
What I need spiritually: _____

Today's Intention: "I acknowledge my needs as valid and important."

Three Self-Acknowledgments:
1. I acknowledge my need for: _____
2. I validate my desire for: _____
3. I accept that I require: _____

Needs Exploration

Basic Needs Inventory:
- ☐ Adequate sleep (hours needed: ___)
- ☐ Regular meals
- ☐ Movement/exercise
- ☐ Quiet time
- ☐ Social connection
- ☐ Creative expression
- ☐ Mental stimulation
- ☐ Emotional support

Unmet Needs Currently:
1. _____
2. _____
3. _____

What Stops Me from Meeting Them:
- ☐ Guilt
- ☐ Time
- ☐ Others' expectations
- ☐ Not feeling deserving
- ☐ Not knowing how

Evening Reflection

Needs Recognition:
Needs I honored today: _____
Needs I ignored: _____
Why: _____
_____

When I Meet My Needs:
I am: _____
Others receive: _____

Guilt vs. Self-Care:
Where guilt arose: _____
Truth about this need: _____

Needs Wisdom

My Top 3 Non-Negotiable Needs:
1. _____
2. _____
3. _____

One Need to Prioritize Tomorrow:
_____
_____
_____

Daily Tracking

- Needs acknowledged: _____
- Needs met: _____
- Guilt level: _____ /10 (lower is better)

Permission Slip:
"I give myself permission to need _____
_____"

Affirmation:
"My needs are not selfish; they're essential."

THE POWER OF NO

Date: ___/___/___ • Day 63 of 90

Today's Theme: *Saying No as Self-Care*
Every yes to others' demands without consideration is a no to yourself.

Morning Practice

No Readiness Check:
Saying no feels:
- ☐ Impossible
- ☐ Difficult
- ☐ Uncomfortable
- ☐ Necessary
- ☐ Empowering
- ☐ Emotional support

Today's 'No' Practice: "I can say no kindly and firmly when needed."

Three Times Saying No Would Have Helped:
1. _____
2. _____
3. _____

'No' Practice Scripts

Polite but Firm No's:
- "Thank you for thinking of me, but I can't commit to that."
- "I appreciate the invitation, but it doesn't work for me."
- "I'm not able to take that on right now."
- "That won't be possible for me."
- "I need to decline."

Your Comfortable Version:
_____
_____
_____

Practice Situation:
Request likely today: _____

Your 'no' response: _____
_____
_____

Evening Reflection

'No' Practice Results:
Times I said no: _____
How it felt: _____
Others' reactions: _____
My response to reactions: _____
_____

Times I Said Yes but Meant No:
Situation: _____
Cost to me: _____
Next time: _____

'No' Wisdom

Saying No Protects:
_____
_____
_____

Saying No Allows:
_____
_____
_____

My No is Valid Because:
_____
_____
_____

Daily Tracking

- No's said clearly: _____
- Yes's that honored me: _____
- Boundary strength: _____ /10

'No' Affirmation:
"My no is complete. It needs no justification."

COMMUNICATING BOUNDARIES

Date: ____ / ____ / ____ • Day 64 of 90

Today's Theme: *Clear, Kind Communication*
Boundaries require communication. Today, practice expressing them clearly.

Morning Practice

Communication Check:
My communication style tends to be:
- ☐ Aggressive
- ☐ Passive
- ☐ Passive-aggressive
- ☐ Assertive

Today's Communication Goal: "I communicate my boundaries clearly, kindly, and firmly."

Boundaries Needing Communication:
1. With: _____ About: _____
2. With: _____ About: _____
3. With: _____ About: _____

Boundary Communication Framework

The Formula:
1. State the boundary: "I need…"
2. Explain briefly (optional): "Because…"
3. Make a request: "Please…"
4. Confirm understanding: "Does that work?"

Example Applications:

Time Boundary:
"I need to end work calls by 6pm. This helps me maintain balance. Please schedule within work hours. Does that work?"

Emotional Boundary:
"I need conversations to stay respectful. Please avoid raising voices. Can we agree on that?"

Your Practice:
Boundary: _____
Script: _____
_____
_____

Evening Reflection

Communication Practice:
Boundaries communicated: _____
Method used: _____
Reception: _____

Clarity Assessment:
Was I clear? Yes/No
Was I kind? Yes/No
Was I firm? Yes/No

Communication Insights:
What worked: _____
What to adjust: _____

Communication Growth

Old Pattern: _____
_____

New Pattern: _____
_____

Tomorrow's Communication:
_____
_____
_____

Daily Tracking

- Boundaries communicated: _____
- Clarity level: _____ /10
- Self-advocacy: _____ /10

Communication Affirmation:
"I can express my needs and boundaries with clarity and compassion."

MAINTAINING BOUNDARIES

Date: ___/___/___ • Day 65 of 90

Today's Theme: *Consistency in Boundary Keeping*
Setting boundaries is step one. Maintaining them requires consistent reinforcement.

Morning Practice

Maintenance Check:
Boundaries that slip: _____
Why they slip: _____

Cost of slippage: _____

Today's Maintenance Focus: "I maintain my boundaries even when challenged."

Three Boundaries to Reinforce:
1. _____
2. _____
3. _____

Boundary Maintenance Strategies

When Boundaries Are Tested:

The Broken Record: Repeat your boundary calmly without justifying.

The Redirect: "We discussed this. My boundary remains…"

The Consequence: "If this continues, I'll need to…"

The Exit: "I'm going to step away now."

Your Go-To Strategy:
_____
_____
_____

Preparation for Pushback:
Common pushback: _____
Your response: _____
_____
_____

Evening Reflection

Maintenance Practice:
Boundaries tested today: _____
How I responded: _____
Boundary held? Yes/No/Partially

When I Wavered:
Why: _____
_____

Cost: _____
Lesson: _____

Boundary Strength

Boundaries Growing Stronger:
_____
_____
_____

Boundaries Still Fragile:
_____
_____
_____

Support I Need:
_____
_____
_____

Daily Tracking

- Boundaries maintained: _____
- Challenges navigated: _____
- Consistency: _____ /10

Maintenance Affirmation:
"My boundaries deserve consistent respect, especially from me."

SELF-CARE AS A NEED

Date: ____ / ____ / ____ • Day 66 of 90

Today's Theme: *Self-Care Isn't Selfish*

Self-care is meeting your own needs so you can show up fully in life.

Morning Practice

Self-Care Assessment:
Physical self-care: _____ /10
Emotional self-care: _____ /10
Mental self-care: _____ /10
Spiritual self-care: _____ /10

Today's Self-Care Commitment: "Meeting my needs through self-care is an act of self-respect."

Three Self-Care Needs:
1. My body needs: _____
2. My mind needs: _____
3. My spirit needs: _____

Boundary Maintenance Strategies

Daily Minimums:
- ☐ Sleep: _____ hours
- ☐ Meals: _____ nutritious
- ☐ Movement: _____ minutes
- ☐ Quiet time: _____ minutes
- ☐ Connection: _____ meaningful

This Week's Self-Care:
Monday: _____
Tuesday: _____
Wednesday: _____
Thursday: _____
Friday: _____
Weekend: _____

One Non-Negotiable:
_____
_____
_____

Evening Reflection

Self-Care Provided:
Morning care: _____
Afternoon care: _____
Evening care: _____

Impact of Self-Care:
Energy: _____
Mood: _____
Capacity for others: _____

Self-Care Wisdom

Self-Care Is Not:
- Selfish
- Luxury
- Reward for productivity
- Only when convenient

Self-Care Is:
- Necessary
- Preventative
- Daily practice
- Self-respect in action

My Self-Care Truth:
_____
_____
_____

Daily Tracking

- Self-care actions: _____
- Needs met: _____ /10
- Energy sustained: _____ /10

Self-Care Affirmation:
"Caring for myself enables me to care for others from fullness, not depletion."

WEEK 5 INTEGRATION

Date: ____/____/____ • Day 67 of 90

Today's Theme: *Celebrating Boundaries and Needs*

Five weeks of practice! You're learning to protect your peace and honor your needs.

Morning Practice

Week 5 Reflection:
Boundaries identified: _____
Needs acknowledged: _____
No's practiced: _____
Growth experienced: _____

Integration Intention: "I celebrate my growing ability to honor my boundaries and meet my needs."

Three Boundary Victories:
1. _____
2. _____
3. _____

Week 5 Harvest

Boundaries & Needs Tools:
- ☐ Boundary awareness   ☐ No practice   ☐ Consistent maintenance
- ☐ Needs identification ☐ Clear communication   ☐ Self-care priority

Biggest Boundary Win: _____
Most Important Need Recognized: _____
Relationships Improving Because: _____

Evening Integration

Days completed: 67/90   Needs awareness: ____ /10
Boundary strength: ____ /10   Self-advocacy: ____ /10

Five-Week Transformation:
Week 1: Awareness → _____
Week 2: Challenging thoughts → _____
Week 3: Body compassion → _____
Week 4: Emotional acceptance → _____
Week 5: Boundaries & needs → _____

What's Different:
How I protect myself: _____
How I honor needs: _____
How I communicate: _____

Week 5 Summary

Average daily ratings:
• Forgiveness capacity: ____ /10 • Needs met: ____ /10 • Self-respect: ____ /10

Message to Week 6 Self: _____

Week 5 Affirmation: "I have spent 67 days building self-love through awareness, compassion, and now boundaries. I am becoming who I've always been."

Celebration: How will you honor five weeks? _____

Continue to Week 6 ⟶

Letting Go to Move Forward

Forgiveness & Release

Days 68-74 of Your Practice

This week's focus: Learning to forgive yourself and others, releasing what no longer serves you, and creating space for growth.

Forgiveness isn't about condoning harmful behavior or forgetting boundaries. It's about freeing yourself from the weight of resentment, guilt, and old stories. This week, you'll practice letting go with compassion.

Week 6 Intentions

- Practice self-forgiveness for past mistakes
- Release guilt and shame that no longer serve
- Let go of perfectionism and impossible standards
- Process resentments with compassion
- Create space for new growth

Understanding Forgiveness

Forgiveness is:
- Releasing the burden of anger
- Choosing peace over being right
- Freeing your energy for the present
- An act of self-care
- A process, not a moment

This Week's Foundation

"I release what weighs me down. Forgiveness sets me free."

SELF-FORGIVENESS INVENTORY ──────────────

Date: ____ / ____ / ____   • Day 68 of 90

Today's Theme: *What Needs Forgiving*
Before we can forgive, we must acknowledge what we're holding against ourselves

Morning Practice

Forgiveness Readiness:
My willingness to forgive myself: ____ /10
My resistance level: ____ /10
What I fear about forgiving: _____
_____

Today's Intention: "I explore what needs forgiveness with gentleness and honesty."

Three Gratitudes for Mistakes: (They taught you something)
1. _____
2. _____
3. _____

Self-Forgiveness Inventory

What I Hold Against Myself:
Past Mistakes:
- ☐ Relationship choices
- ☐ Career decisions
- ☐ Words spoken/unspoken
- ☐ Opportunities missed
- ☐ Harm caused to others
- ☐ Harm caused to self
- ☐ Time "wasted"

Specific Regrets:
1. _____
2. _____
3. _____

The Heaviest Burden:
_____
_____
_____

How Long I've Carried This:
_____
_____

Month 2 • Week 6: Forgiveness & Release

Evening Reflection

Inventory Insights:
What surprised me: _____
What felt heaviest: _____
What's ready for release: _____

The Cost of Not Forgiving:
Emotionally: _____
Physically: _____
Relationally: _____

If I Forgave Myself:
I would feel: _____
I could: _____

Forgiveness Readiness

What Feels Forgivable:
_____
_____
_____

What Feels Harder:
_____
_____
_____

One Small Thing to Start:
_____
_____
_____

Daily Tracking

- Self-criticisms noticed: _____
- Compassion offered: _____
- Readiness growing: _____ /10

Tomorrow's Focus:
_____
_____
_____

Affirmation:
"I am ready to explore forgiveness as an act of self-love."

UNDERSTANDING WHY

Date: ____/____/____ • Day 69 of 90

Today's Theme: *Context and Compassion*
Every mistake had a context. Understanding why helps forgiveness flow.

Morning Practice

Context Check:
When I made that mistake, I was: _____
What I didn't know then: _____
What I was trying to do: _____

Today's Intention: "I see my past self with understanding and compassion."

Three Things Past Me Didn't Know:
1. _____
2. _____
3. _____

Understanding Your Past Self

The Mistake: _____

The Context:
- My age/experience: _____
- My emotional state: _____
- My resources: _____
- My support: _____
- My knowledge: _____

What I Was Trying To Do:
- [ ] Protect myself
- [ ] Meet a need
- [ ] Connect with others
- [ ] Survive
- [ ] Be loved
- [ ] Do my best

The Truth Is: "Given everything, I did the best I could with what I knew."

Evening Reflection

Compassionate Understanding:
When I see the full context: _____
I understand that: _____
_____

I can have compassion because: _____
_____

Past Self Wisdom:
They were doing their best: Yes/No
They deserve compassion: Yes/No
They've learned since then: Yes/No

Shifting Perspective

Old Story: "I should have known better"
New Understanding: _____
_____
_____

What Changes When I Understand:
_____
_____
_____

Tomorrow's Forgiveness Work:
_____
_____
_____

Daily Tracking

- Compassion for past self: _____ /10
- Understanding gained: _____ /10
- Story shifting: _____ /10

Compassion Statement:
"My past self deserves understanding for _____
_____"

Affirmation:
"I did the best I could with the awareness I had."

THE FORGIVENESS PROCESS

Date: ____ / ____ / ____ • Day 70 of 90

Today's Theme: *Active Forgiveness Practice*
Today, actively practice forgiving one thing you've held against yourself.

Morning Practice

Choosing What to Forgive:
Today I forgive myself for: _____
I'm ready because: _____
This matters because: _____

Forgiveness Intention: "I release this burden with love and move forward in freedom."

Three Forgiveness Truths:
1. Forgiveness is for me, not them
2. I can forgive and still have boundaries
3. Forgiveness is a process, not perfection

The Forgiveness Ritual

Step 1: Acknowledge
"I acknowledge that I _____"

Step 2: Feel
The emotions present: _____
Where I feel them: _____

Step 3: Understand
"I understand I was _____"

Step 4: Release
"I release the guilt/shame/anger about _____"

Step 5: Replace
"I replace judgment with _____"

Step 6: Commit
"I commit to _____"

Your Forgiveness Statement:
_____
_____
_____

Evening Reflection

Forgiveness Practice Results:
How the ritual felt: _____

What shifted: _____
What remains: _____

Body Response:
Before forgiveness: _____

After forgiveness: _____

Forgiveness in Progress

What Released:
_____
_____
_____

What Needs More Time:
_____
_____
_____

I'm Learning:
_____
_____
_____

Daily Tracking

- Forgiveness practiced: Yes/No
- Release felt: _____ /10
- Peace growing: _____ /10

Forgiveness Progress:
"Today I released _____
_____"

Affirmation:
"Forgiveness is a gift I give myself."

RELEASING PERFECTIONISM

Date: ___/___/___ • Day 71 of 90

Today's Theme: *Letting Go of Impossible Standards*
Perfectionism is self-punishment disguised as self-improvement.

Morning Practice

Choosing What to Forgive:
Areas where I demand perfection: _____
Cost of these standards: _____
What "good enough" would look like: _____
_____

Today's Intention: "I release perfectionism and embrace progress."

Three Places I Can Lower the Bar:
1. _____
2. _____
3. _____

Perfectionism Release

The Perfectionist Says:
"You must be _____"
"You can't make mistakes in _____"
"Others expect _____"

The Truth Is:
"I am human and allowed to _____"
"Mistakes are _____"
"Good enough is _____"

Perfectionism Protects Me From:
☐ Judgment
☐ Rejection
☐ Feeling inadequate
☐ Being seen as flawed
☐ Disappointment

But It Costs Me:
_____
_____
_____

Evening Reflection

Perfectionism Release Practice:
Where I lowered standards: _____
What happened: _____
_____
How it felt: _____

The World Didn't End When:
_____
_____
_____

Freedom From Perfectionism

I'm Learning:
Excellence ≠ Perfection
Progress > Perfection
Done > Perfect

Tomorrow I'll Practice:
_____
_____
_____

Daily Tracking

- Perfectionist thoughts caught: _____
- Standards adjusted: _____
- Self-compassion: _____ /10

Liberation Statement: "I am free to be imperfect and still be worthy."

Affirmation:
"My imperfections make me human, relatable, and real."

FORGIVING OTHERS

Date: ___/___/___ • Day 72 of 90

Today's Theme: *Releasing Resentment*

Forgiving others frees your energy from the past.

Morning Practice

Resentment Inventory:
Who I need to forgive: _____
What I'm holding: _____

How long I've carried this: _____

Today's Intention: "I explore forgiving others for my own peace."

Three Truths About Forgiveness:
1. It doesn't mean condoning behavior
2. It doesn't require reconciliation
3. It's about my freedom, not their absolution

Forgiving Others Process

The Person: _____

What Happened:
_____
_____

How It Affected Me:
_____
_____

What They Might Have Been Experiencing:
_____
_____

What I Wish Had Been Different:
_____
_____

What I'm Ready to Release:
_____
_____

My Forgiveness Statement: "I release my anger about _____ to free myself for peace."

Evening Reflection

Forgiveness Exploration:
What felt possible: _____
What feels stuck: _____
What I learned: _____
_____

Energy Shift:
Before considering forgiveness: _____
After exploring it: _____

Forgiveness Wisdom

Forgiving Others Doesn't Mean:
- They were right
- I have to forget
- Boundaries disappear
- Relationship resumes

It Does Mean:
- I choose peace
- I reclaim my energy
- I stop drinking poison
- I move forward

One Person I Can Start With:
_____
_____

Daily Tracking

- Resentments examined: _____
- Willingness to forgive: _____ /10
- Peace level: _____ /10

Affirmation:
"I forgive others to free myself."

RELEASING OLD STORIES

Date: ___/___/___ • Day 73 of 90

Today's Theme: *Updating Your Narrative*
Old stories about who you are keep you stuck. Time to update them.

Morning Practice

Story Check:
Old story I tell about myself: _____
_____

Evidence it's outdated: _____
_____

New story available: _____
_____

Today's Intention: "I release old stories that no longer serve my growth."

Three Stories Ready for Update:
1. "I am someone who always _____" → "I am learning to _____"
2. "I can't _____" → "I am building skills in _____"
3. "I'm not the type to _____" → "I'm exploring _____"

Forgiving Others Process

Old Story: "I am _____"

Origin: This story came from _____

Evidence Against It:
1. _____
2. _____
3. _____

New Story: "I am _____"

Evidence For It:
1. _____
2. _____
3. _____

Living the New Story Looks Like:
_____
_____

Month 2 • Week 6: Forgiveness & Release | 151

Evening Reflection

Story Release Results:
Old story moments: _____
New story moments: _____
How the shift felt: _____
_____

Identity Updating:
Who I thought I was: _____
Who I'm becoming: _____

New Narrative

Stories Released Today:
_____
_____
_____

Stories Embraced:
_____
_____
_____

Tomorrow's Story:
_____
_____
_____

Daily Tracking

- Old stories noticed: _____
- New stories practiced: _____
- Identity flexibility: _____ /10

Story Affirmation:
"I am the author of my story. I can rewrite any chapter."

WEEK 6 INTEGRATION

Date: ___/___/___ • Day 74 of 90

Today's Theme: *Celebrating Release and Renewal*

Six weeks complete! You've learned to forgive, release, and create space for growth.

Morning Practice

Week 6 Reflection:
What I forgave: _____
What I released: _____
What I updated: _____
How I feel: _____

Integration Intention: "I celebrate my courage to forgive and my wisdom to release."

Three Things I'm No Longer Carrying:
1. _____
2. _____
3. _____

Week 6 Harvest

Forgiveness & Release Tools:
- ☐ Self-forgiveness practice
- ☐ Context and compassion
- ☐ Active forgiveness ritual
- ☐ Perfectionism release
- ☐ Forgiving others
- ☐ Story updating

Biggest Release: _____
Biggest Boundary Win: _____
Most Important Need Recognized: _____

Evening Integration

Days completed: 74/90   Emotional freedom: ___ /10
Forgiveness capacity: ___ /10   Story flexibility: ___ /10

Six-Week Journey:
Started with: _____
Arriving at: _____
Growing into: _____

What's Different:
How I treat my past: _____
How I hold mistakes: _____
How I see myself: _____

Week 6 Summary

Average daily ratings:
- Forgiveness capacity: ___ /10
- Release achieved: ___ /10
- Peace growing: ___ /10

Message to Week 7 Self: _____

Week 6 Affirmation: "Through forgiveness and release, I create space for joy and growth."

Celebration: How will you honor this release? _____

Continue to Week 7 ⟶

**Cultivating Positive Emotions
and Acknowledging Growth**

Joy & Celebration

Days 75-81 of Your Practice

This week's focus: Actively creating joy, celebrating progress, and building positive emotional experiences to balance the deeper work you've done.

After six weeks of awareness, challenge, and release, it's time to intentionally cultivate joy. This isn't toxic positivity—it's balanced emotional nourishment. You've created space through forgiveness; now fill it with celebration.

Week 7 Intentions

- Notice and amplify existing joy moments
- Create intentional joy practices
- Celebrate progress without minimizing
- Build gratitude as a daily practice
- Share joy with others

Understanding Joy

Joy is:
- Available even in difficulty
- Not dependent on perfection
- A practice, not just a feeling
- Multiplied when shared
- Your birthright

This Week's Foundation

"I deserve joy. I create celebration. I amplify the good."

JOY INVENTORY

Date: ____ / ____ / ____ • Day 75 of 90

Today's Theme: *Recognizing What Brings Joy*

Before creating more joy, notice what already sparks it

Morning Practice

Joy Check:
Current joy level: ____ /10
Last moment of genuine joy: _____
What I was doing: _____
_____

Today's Intention: "I notice and appreciate moments of joy, however small."

Three Recent Joys: (Even tiny ones count)
1. _____
2. _____
3. _____

Joy Exploration

What Consistently Brings Joy:

Simple Pleasures:
- ☐ Morning coffee/tea
- ☐ Sunshine on skin
- ☐ Favorite song
- ☐ Pet snuggles
- ☐ Good book
- ☐ Laughter
- ☐ Movement
- ☐ Creating

Deeper Joys:
Connection with: _____
Accomplishing: _____
Experiencing: _____
Contributing: _____

Joy Surprises:
Unexpected joy from: _____

What Blocks My Joy:
- ☐ Guilt about feeling good
- ☐ Waiting for "perfect" conditions
- ☐ Fear it won't last
- ☐ Comparison to others
- ☐ Old programming

Evening Reflection

Joy Noticed Today:
Morning joy: _____
Afternoon joy: _____
Evening joy: _____

When I Paid Attention:
Joy was:
- ☐ More frequent
- ☐ More intense
- ☐ More accessible
- ☐ Emotional support

Joy Insights:
I find joy in: _____
Joy comes easier when: _____

Forgiveness Wisdom

My Joy Signature:
Types of joy I gravitate toward: _____
_____
_____

Untapped Joy Sources:
_____
_____
_____

Tomorrow's Joy Intention:
_____
_____
_____

Daily Tracking

- Joy moments noticed: _____
- Joy intensity average: _____ /10
- Joy shared: Yes/No

Joy Discovery:
"I'm learning that joy _____
_____"

Affirmation:
"Joy is always available to me, even in small doses."

156 | Month 2 • Week 7: Joy & Celebration

CELEBRATING PROGRESS

Date: ____/____/____ • Day 76 of 90

Today's Theme: *Acknowledging How Far You've Come*
Celebration isn't waiting until you're "done"—it's recognizing every step.

Morning Practice

Progress Check:
Where I started (Day 1): _____

Where I am now: _____

Growth I see: _____

Today's Intention: "I celebrate my progress without minimizing or comparing."

Three Wins This Journey: (Any size)
1. _____
2. _____
3. _____

Celebration Practice

Micro-Victories from This Week:
- ☐ Said no to something
- ☐ Honored a need
- ☐ Caught critical thought
- ☐ Practiced self-care
- ☐ Set a boundary
- ☐ Chose self-compassion
- ☐ Other: _____

Bigger Victories:
Month 1: _____

Month 2 so far: _____

What I'm Proud Of:
The courage to: _____
The persistence to: _____
The compassion to: _____

How Past Me Would See Current Me:
_____
_____
_____

Evening Reflection

Celebration Practiced:
What I celebrated: _____
How I celebrated: _____
How it felt: _____

Resistance to Celebrating:
Came up when: _____
Sounded like: _____
I responded with: _____

Celebration Wisdom

Celebrating Progress:
- Doesn't mean I'm done
- Motivates continuation
- Rewires for positivity
- Validates effort

My Celebration Style:
_____
_____
_____

Tomorrow I'll Celebrate:
_____
_____
_____

Daily Tracking

- Victories acknowledged: _____
- Celebration acts: _____
- Pride level: _____ /10

Celebration Statement:
"I am _____ and that deserves celebration."

Affirmation:
"Every step forward deserves recognition."

CREATING JOY

Date: ____/____/____ • Day 77 of 90

Today's Theme: *Intentional Joy Creation*

Don't wait for joy to find you—actively create it.

Morning Practice

Joy Creation Plan:
One joyful thing I'll do today: _____
Time I'll do it: _____
Why this brings joy: _____
_____

Today's Intention: "I actively create moments of joy in my day."

Three Ways to Add Joy:
1. _____
2. _____
3. _____

Joy Creation Menu

5-Minute Joy:
- ☐ Dance to favorite song
- ☐ Text someone love
- ☐ Look at happy photos
- ☐ Step outside
- ☐ Stretch with pleasure
- ☐ Savor a treat

15-Minute Joy:
- ☐ Call a friend
- ☐ Take joy walk
- ☐ Create something
- ☐ Play
- ☐ Listen to comedy
- ☐ Practice hobby

30+ Minute Joy:
- ☐ Extended creative time
- ☐ Nature immersion
- ☐ Celebration meal
- ☐ Joy date with self
- ☐ Share activity with loved one

Today's Joy Choice:
_____
_____
_____

Evening Reflection

Joy Created Today:
Intentional joy moments: _____
_____

Spontaneous joy: _____
_____

Total joy minutes: _____

Creation Impact:
Energy level: _____
Mood shift: _____
Ripple effects: _____
_____

Joy Expansion

What Worked:
_____
_____
_____

What to Try Tomorrow:
_____
_____
_____

Joy Multiplier:
When I shared joy: _____
_____
_____

Daily Tracking

- Joy actively created: _____ times
- Joy minutes total: _____
- Energy boost: _____ /10

Joy Learning:
"Creating joy makes me _____"

Affirmation:
"I am the architect of my own joy."

GRATITUDE PRACTICE ─────────────

Date: ____ / ____ / ____ • Day 78 of 90

Today's Theme: *Intentional Joy Creation*
Deepening Gratitude

Morning Practice

Gratitude Depth:
Surface gratitude: "I'm grateful for coffee"
Deeper gratitude: "I'm grateful for the warmth, ritual, and pause coffee provides"

Today's Deep Gratitudes:
1. Surface: _____ Deeper: _____
2. Surface: _____ Deeper: _____
3. Surface: _____ Deeper: _____

Today's Intention: "I practice gratitude that touches my heart."

Gratitude Expansion

Gratitude Categories:
For My Journey:
_____

For My Body:
_____

For My Support:
_____

For My Challenges: (Yes, even these)
_____

For Simple Things:
_____

Unexpected Gratitude:
_____

Gratitude Letter: (To yourself or someone else)
Dear _____ ,
_____
_____
_____
_____

Evening Reflection

Gratitude Practice Results:
Morning gratitudes: _____
Noticed throughout day: _____
Evening appreciation: _____

When I Practice Gratitude:
I notice: _____
_____
I feel: _____
Others notice: _____

Gratitude Impact

Shift in Perspective:
From lack to: _____
From criticism to: _____

Gratitude Habit Forming:
Ease today: _____ /10
Natural moments: _____

Daily Tracking

- Gratitudes expressed: _____
- Depth reached: _____ /10
- Heart touched: _____ /10

Gratitude Discovery:
_____
_____
_____

Affirmation:
"Gratitude is my gateway to joy and abundance."

SHARING JOY

Date: ___/___/___ • Day 79 of 90

Today's Theme: *Joy Multiplied Through Connection*
Joy shared is joy doubled. Today, spread your light.

Morning Practice

Sharing Readiness:
Comfort sharing joy: _____ /10
Fear about sharing: _____
Person to share with: _____

Today's Intention: "I share my joy freely, multiplying positivity."

Three Ways to Share Joy:
1. _____
2. _____
3. _____

Joy Sharing Practice

Ways to Share:

Quick Shares:
- ☐ Smile genuinely
- ☐ Compliment someone
- ☐ Share good news
- ☐ Send appreciative text
- ☐ Offer help gladly

Deeper Shares:
- ☐ Celebrate someone else
- ☐ Share your progress
- ☐ Express gratitude directly
- ☐ Invite someone to joy activity
- ☐ Create something for someone

Today's Sharing Plan:
Who: _____
What: _____
How: _____

Without Diminishing: "I can share joy without downplaying it"

Evening Reflection

Joy Shared Today:
What I shared: _____
With whom: _____
Their response: _____
How it felt: _____

Joy Multiplication:
My joy level before sharing: _____ /10
After sharing: _____ /10

Gratitude Impact

Sharing Joy Taught Me:
_____
_____
_____

Resistance Encountered:
_____
_____
_____

Tomorrow's Share:
_____
_____
_____

Daily Tracking

- Joy moments shared: _____
- Connections deepened: _____
- Joy amplification: _____ /10

Sharing Affirmation:
"My joy is meant to be shared and celebrated."

SUSTAINABLE JOY

Date: ___/___/___ • Day 80 of 90

Today's Theme: *Building Lasting Joy Practices*
Create joy practices that sustain you beyond this journey.

Morning Practice

Sustainable Joy Check:
What joy practices feel sustainable: _____
What feels forced: _____
My natural joy rhythm: _____

Today's Intention: "I build sustainable joy practices that fit my real life."

Three Joy Practices to Keep:
1. Daily: _____
2. Weekly: _____
3. Monthly: _____

Sustainable Joy Blueprint

Morning Joy Ritual: (5 minutes)
_____
_____

Workday Joy Breaks:
When: _____
What: _____

Evening Joy Practice:
_____
_____

Weekly Joy Commitment:
Day: _____
Activity: _____
Duration: _____

Monthly Joy Celebration:
_____
_____

Joy Emergency Kit: (For hard days)
1. _____
2. _____
3. _____

Evening Reflection

Sustainable Practice Test:
What felt natural: _____

What felt forced: _____

What to adjust: _____

Joy Sustainability Factors:
- Must be simple
- Must be accessible
- Must be flexible
- Must be genuine

Building Lasting Joy

My Joy Non-Negotiables:
_____
_____
_____

My Joy Flexibility:
_____
_____
_____

Support Needed:
_____
_____
_____

Daily Tracking

- Sustainable practices identified: _____
- Ease of implementation: _____ /10
- Commitment level: _____ /10

Sustainability Promise:
"I commit to sustainable joy practices that nourish me daily."

WEEK 7 INTEGRATION

Date: ___/___/___ • Day 81 of 90

Today's Theme: *Celebrating Joy as Medicine*

Seven weeks! You've moved from awareness through release into active joy creation.

Morning Practice

Week 7 Reflection:
Joy discovered: _____
Progress celebrated: _____
Joy created: _____
Joy shared: _____

Integration Intention: "I celebrate my capacity for joy and my commitment to cultivation."

Three Joy Victories:
1. _____
2. _____
3. _____

Week 7 Harvest

Joy & Celebration Tools:
☐ Joy inventory   ☐ Active joy creation   ☐ Joy sharing
☐ Progress celebration   ☐ Gratitude deepening   ☐ Sustainable practices

Biggest Joy Discovery: _____
Most Powerful Celebration: _____
Joy Practice to Keep Forever: _____

Evening Integration

Days completed: 81/90   Celebration comfort: ___ /10
Joy capacity: ___ /10   Gratitude depth: ___ /10

Seven-Week Transformation:

Week 1: Built awareness   Week 5: Set boundaries
Week 2: Challenged thoughts   Week 6: Released burdens
Week 3: Embraced body   Week 7: Created joy
Week 4: Accepted emotions

What's Different:
How I experience joy: _____
How I hold mistakes: _____
How I see myself: _____

Week 7 Summary

Average daily ratings:
• Forgiveness capacity: ___ /10   • Celebration practice: ___ /10
• Gratitude depth: ___ /10

Message to Week 8 Self: _____

Week 7 Affirmation: "I have spent 81 days transforming my relationship with myself. Joy is my birthright and celebration is my practice."
Celebration: How will you celebrate seven weeks? _____

Continue to Week 8 ⟶

Bringing It All Together

Integration

Days 82–88 of Your Practice

This week's focus: Synthesizing eight weeks of practice into a sustainable, personalized approach to self-love that fits your real life.

You've built awareness, challenged thoughts, embraced your body, accepted emotions, set boundaries, released burdens, and cultivated joy. Now it's time to weave these threads into a tapestry you can live with daily.

Week 8 Intentions

- Identify what practices serve you most
- Create your personalized toolkit
- Build sustainable daily rhythms
- Prepare for independent practice
- Celebrate your transformation

Integration Understanding

Integration means:
- Keeping what works
- Releasing what doesn't
- Adapting to your life
- Creating sustainability
- Honoring your growth

This Week's Foundation

"I take what serves me and create a practice that sustains me."

PRACTICE INVENTORY ———————————————

Date: ____ / ____ / ____ • Day 82 of 90

Today's Theme: *Identifying What Works*
After 81 days, you know what resonates. Time to claim your practices.

Morning Practice

Practice Review:
Most helpful practice: _____
Most challenging: _____
Most surprising: _____

Today's Intention: "I identify the practices that truly serve my wellbeing."

Three Practices I'll Keep Forever:
1. _____
2. _____
3. _____

Practice Assessment

Week by Week Review:

Week 1 (Awareness):
Keep: _____ Modify: _____ Release: _____

Week 2 (Challenging):
Keep: _____ Modify: _____ Release: _____

Week 3 (Body):
Keep: _____ Modify: _____ Release: _____

Week 4 (Emotions):
Keep: _____ Modify: _____ Release: _____

Week 5 (Boundaries):
Keep: _____ Modify: _____ Release: _____

Week 6 (Forgiveness):
Keep: _____ Modify: _____ Release: _____

Week 7 (Joy):
Keep: _____ Modify: _____ Release: _____

My Core Practices:
Daily: _____
Weekly: _____
As needed: _____

Evening Reflection

Practice Clarity:
What I definitely keep: _____
What needs adjustment: _____
What I can release: _____

Practice Criteria:
Works when: _____
_____

Doesn't when: _____
_____

Your Practice Signature

I Thrive With
- ☐ Morning rituals
- ☐ Evening reflection
- ☐ Quick check-ins
- ☐ Longer sessions
- ☐ Written practice
- ☐ Movement practice
- ☐ Creative practice

My Style Is:
_____
_____
_____

Daily Tracking

- Practices reviewed: _____
- Clarity gained: _____ /10
- Confidence in choices: _____ /10

Integration Insight:
"My practice works best when _____"

Affirmation:
"I know what serves me and choose accordingly."

YOUR PERSONAL TOOLKIT ────────────────────

Date: ____ / ____ / ____ • Day 83 of 90

Today's Theme: *Building Your Custom Toolkit*

Create your personalized collection of tools for different situations.

Morning Practice

Toolkit Inventory:
Most used tool: _____
Most effective: _____
Emergency go-to: _____

Today's Intention: "I create a toolkit that supports me in all situations."

My Essential Tools:
1. _____
2. _____
3. _____

Your Custom Toolkit

For Daily Practice:
Morning tool: _____
Midday tool: _____
Evening tool: _____

For Challenges:
When anxious: _____
When critical: _____
When overwhelmed: _____

For Growth:
Boundary tool: _____
Self-compassion tool: _____
Joy creation tool: _____

For Emergencies:
Quick reset: _____
Deep support: _____
Connection tool: _____

Evening Reflection

Toolkit Testing:
What I used today: _____
How it worked: _____
What I'd adjust: _____

Tool Effectiveness:
Most versatile: _____
Most powerful: _____
Most accessible: _____

Your Toolkit Blueprint

Daily Essentials: (5 min)
_____
_____
_____

Weekly Practices: (20 min)
_____
_____
_____

Monthly Check-ins: (30 min)
_____
_____
_____

Daily Tracking

- Tools identified: _____
- Toolkit clarity: _____ /10
- Confidence in tools: _____ /10

Integration Insight:
"My most essential tool is _____"

Affirmation:
"I have all the tools I need for my journey."

DAILY RHYTHMS ─────────────────────────────

Date: ___/___/___ • Day 84 of 90

Today's Theme: *Creating Sustainable Daily Practice*
Design rhythms that fit your real life.

Morning Practice

Current Rhythms:
Morning routine: _____
Evening routine: _____
Best practice time: _____

Today's Intention: "I create sustainable rhythms that nourish me daily."

Non-Negotiables:
1. _____
2. _____
3. _____

Rhythm Design

Morning Practice: (_____ minutes)
☐ _____
☐ _____
☐ _____

Midday Reset: (_____ minutes)
☐ _____
☐ _____

Evening Practice: (_____ minutes)
☐ _____
☐ _____
☐ _____

Weekly Deepening:
Day: _____
Practice: _____
Time: _____
Duration: _____

Monthly Reflection:
Date: _____
Focus: _____

Evening Reflection

Rhythm Reality Check:
What felt natural: _____
What felt forced: _____
What to adjust: _____

Sustainability Factors:
Works with my schedule: _____ /10
Feels manageable: _____ /10
Brings me joy: _____ /10

Your Rhythm Commitment

I Commit To:
Daily minimum: _____ minutes
Weekly deepening: _____ minutes
Monthly reflection: _____ minutes

My Rhythm Anchors:
Morning: _____
Midday: _____
Evening: _____

Daily Tracking

- Rhythms tested: _____
- Flow experienced: _____ /10
- Sustainability confidence: _____ /10

Integration Insight:
"My natural rhythm is _____"

Affirmation:
"I honor my rhythms and create sustainable practice."

SUPPORT SYSTEMS ————————————————————

Date: ____ / ____ / ____ • Day 85 of 90

Today's Theme: *Building Your Support Network*

No journey happens alone. Identify your support systems.

Morning Practice

Current Support:
Internal resources: _____
External support: _____
Professional help: _____

Today's Intention: "I acknowledge and strengthen my support systems."

My Support Team:
1. _____
2. _____
3. _____

Support Mapping

Internal Support:
- ☐ Self-compassion practice
- ☐ Affirmation library
- ☐ Toolkit mastery
- ☐ Boundary skills
- ☐ Joy practices
- ☐ Other: _____

External Support:
- ☐ Trusted friend: _____
- ☐ Family member: _____
- ☐ Professional: _____
- ☐ Community: _____
- ☐ Online resources: _____

Support Activation:
When to reach out: _____
How to ask: _____
What to request: _____

Month 2 • Week 8: Integration | 175

Evening Reflection

Support Assessment:
Support used today: _____
Support needed: _____
Support to strengthen: _____

Connection Quality:
Internal support: _____ /10
External support: _____ /10
Balance between both: _____ /10

Your Support Plan

Daily Support:
Self-check: _____
Connection: _____

Weekly Support:
Check-in with: _____
Community: _____

Emergency Support:
Contact: _____
Alternative: _____
Professional: _____

Daily Tracking

- Support identified: _____
- Connection felt: _____ /10
- Support confidence: _____ /10

Integration Insight:
"I am supported by _____"

Affirmation:
"I am worthy of support and know how to receive it."

OBSTACLES & SOLUTIONS

Date: ____ / ____ / ____ • Day 86 of 90

Today's Theme: *Preparing for Real-Life Challenges*
Anticipate obstacles and create strategies for maintaining practice.

Morning Practice

Obstacle Awareness:
Likely challenges: _____
Past patterns: _____
Current vulnerabilities: _____

Today's Intention: "I prepare wisely for challenges while trusting my resilience."

Three Probable Obstacles:

1. _____
2. _____
3. _____

Obstacle Planning

Common Challenges:

Time Pressure
Solution: _____
Minimum practice: _____

Energy Depletion
Solution: _____
Gentle option: _____

Old Patterns Returning
Solution: _____
Reset practice: _____

Life Stress/Crisis
Solution: _____
Emergency plan: _____

Motivation Dips
Solution: _____
Reconnection practice: _____

Evening Reflection

Challenge Preparedness:
Solutions created: _____
Confidence level: _____ /10
Additional needs: _____

Resilience Resources:
Internal: _____
_____

External: _____
_____

Overcoming Strategy

When I Stumble:
1. Remember: _____
2. Practice: _____
3. Reach out to: _____

Reset Ritual:
_____
_____
_____

Daily Tracking

- Obstacles identified: _____
- Solutions created: _____
- Preparedness: _____ /10

Obstacle Wisdom:
"I can navigate challenges with _____"

Affirmation:
"I have tools for every situation and the wisdom to use them."

FUTURE VISIONING ───────────────────

Date: ____/____/____ • Day 87 of 90

Today's Theme: *Creating Your Continued Path*
Envision your ongoing self-love journey beyond these 90 days.

Morning Practice

Future Vision:
In 3 months: _____

In 6 months: _____

In 1 year: _____

Today's Intention: "I envision and create my continued growth path."

Three Future Commitments:
1. I will maintain: _____
2. I will develop: _____
3. I will explore: _____

Continued Growth Plan

Next 30 Days:
Focus: _____
Daily practice: _____
Weekly practice: _____
Monthly review: _____

Next Quarter:
Growth edge: _____
New exploration: _____
Support needed: _____

Next Year:
Vision: _____
Milestones: _____
Celebrations: _____

Life Vision:
The person I'm becoming: _____

The life I'm creating: _____

Evening Integration

88 Days of Transformation:
Days completed: 88/90
Integration achieved: _____ /10
Self-love embodied: _____ /10
Ready to continue: _____ /10

Eight-Week Journey:
Started with: _____
Arrived at: _____
Continuing toward: _____

What's Permanent:
- How I speak to myself: _____
_____
- How I treat myself: _____
_____
- How I value myself: _____
_____

Final Preparation

Ready for Completion:
What to celebrate: _____
What to release: _____
What to continue: _____

Message to Day 90 Self:
_____
_____

Week 8 Affirmation: "I have successfully integrated 88 days of practice into a sustainable approach to self-love that is uniquely mine."

Integration Celebration: How will you honor this integration? _____
_____

Continue to Days 89-90 ⟶

Completion & Beyond

Days 89-90 of Your Practice and Your On-Going Journey

REFLECTION & GRATITUDE

Date: ___/___/___ • Day 89 of 90

Today's Theme: *Honoring Your Journey*

Tomorrow you complete 90 days. Today, reflect on the profound work you've done.

Morning Practice

Journey Reflection:
I began this journey feeling: _____
I'm approaching completion feeling: _____
The biggest change has been: _____

Gratitude Intention: "I honor my journey with deep gratitude for my commitment and growth."

My Deepest Gratitudes:
1. _____
2. _____
3. _____

Complete Journey Review

Foundation Phase (Days 1-30):
Most impactful lesson: _____
Biggest challenge overcome: _____
Key discovery: _____

Practice Phase (Days 31-60):
Most powerful practice: _____
Greatest breakthrough: _____
Surprising growth: _____

Integration Phase (Days 61-90):
What I integrated: _____
What I released: _____
What I embraced: _____

Gratitude Inventory

I Am Grateful For:

The Challenges:
They taught me: _____

The Breakthroughs:
They showed me: _____

The Difficult Days:
They proved: _____

The Joyful Days:
They reminded me: _____

The Support:
Internal: _____
External: _____

The Growth:
Expected: _____
Unexpected: _____

Evening Reflection

Letter of Thanks to Myself:
_____
_____
_____
_____
_____
_____
_____
_____

Gratitude Practice Forward:
Daily: _____
Weekly: _____
Special occasions: _____

Daily Tracking

- Gratitude expressed: _____
- Fullness felt: _____ /10
- Peace experienced: _____ /10

Gratitude Wisdom:
"This journey has given me _____"

Affirmation:
"I am grateful for who I was, who I am, and who I'm becoming."

COMPLETION CEREMONY

Date: ___/___/___ • Day 90 of 90

Completion Day
You Did It! 90 Days of Self-Love Practice

Today's Theme: *Honoring Your Completion & New Beginning*
This isn't an ending—it's a graduation into self-directed practice

Morning Ceremony

Completion Reflection:
I started because: _____

I continued because: _____

I completed because: _____

Today's Intention: "I honor my completion and embrace my new beginning."

My Completion Declaration:
"This journey has given me _____"

Transformation Assessment

Day 1 vs. Day 90:

Self-Love: Day 1: _____ /10 → Day 90: _____ /10
Self-Compassion: Day 1: _____ /10 → Day 90: _____ /10
Self-Criticism: Day 1: _____ /10 → Day 90: _____ /10
Inner Peace: Day 1: _____ /10 → Day 90: _____ /10
Joy Capacity: Day 1: _____ /10 → Day 90: _____ /10

Practices Mastered:
- ☐ Self-awareness
- ☐ Challenging critical thoughts
- ☐ Body compassion
- ☐ Emotional acceptance
- ☐ Boundary setting
- ☐ Forgiveness & release
- ☐ Joy cultivation
- ☐ Sustainable integration

Most Important Discovery:
_____
_____
_____

Your Graduation Portfolio

Skills Developed:
1. _____
2. _____
3. _____
4. _____
5. _____

Patterns Released:
1. _____
2. _____
3. _____

New Habits Created:
1. _____
2. _____
3. _____

Tools Mastered:
1. _____
2. _____
3. _____

Evening Reflection

Going Forward I Promise:

To Myself:
_____
_____

My Daily Practice:
_____
_____

My Weekly Practice:
_____
_____

My Monthly Check-in:
_____
_____

My Quarterly Review:
_____
_____
_____

Letter to Your Future Self

Write a Letter to Yourself to Open in 90 Days

Dear Future Me (to read on _____),

What I want you to remember about this journey:
_____
_____
_____
_____

The practices I hope you're still doing:
_____
_____
_____

What I learned that I never want to forget:
_____
_____
_____

If you're struggling, remember:
_____
_____
_____

The tools that work best for you are:
_____
_____

You are enough because:
_____
_____
_____
_____

I'm proud of you for:
_____
_____

Keep growing, keep loving yourself, and remember this journey is lifelong.

With love and pride,

_____ (Signature)

Date: _____

YOUR ONGOING PRACTICE PLAN

Creating Your Sustainable Practice

Daily Minimums: (Non-Negotiable)
- ☐ Morning check-in (2 min): _____
- ☐ Evening reflection (3 min): _____
- ☐ One self-compassion act: _____

Weekly Practices:
- ☐ Monday: _____
- ☐ Tuesday: _____
- ☐ Wednesday: _____
- ☐ Thursday: _____
- ☐ Friday: _____
- ☐ Weekend: _____

Monthly Rituals:
- ☐ First Sunday: Deep reflection
- ☐ Mid-month: Progress check
- ☐ Month-end: Celebration practice

Quarterly Reviews:
- ☐ 3 months (Date: _____): Practice assessment
- ☐ 6 months (Date: _____): Mid-year review
- ☐ 9 months (Date: _____): Growth evaluation
- ☐ 12 months (Date: _____): Annual celebration

Emergency Protocol:
When I notice old patterns:

1. _____
2. _____
3. _____

Celebration Plan:
How I'll celebrate milestones: _____
_____
_____
_____

Completion & Beyond

Certificate of Completion

This certifies that

_____

has successfully completed

The 90-Day Self-Love Breakthrough

Through dedication, courage, and commitment, you have transformed your relationship with yourself.

You have learned to:

- Observe with awareness rather than judgment
- Respond with compassion rather than criticism
- Honor your body with kindness
- Accept your emotions with grace
- Set boundaries with confidence
- Release what no longer serves you
- Cultivate joy intentionally
- Create sustainable practice

Date Completed: _____

Signature: _____

Your Affirmation

"I am enough, exactly as I am. My journey of self-love continues with wisdom, tools, and deep self-compassion."

RESOURCES FOR CONTINUED GROWTH

Your Support Library

Books to Explore:
- [ ] Self-Compassion" by Kristin Neff
- [ ] "Radical Acceptance" by Tara Brach
- [ ] "The Gifts of Imperfection" by Brené Brown
- [ ] "When Things Fall Apart" by Pema Chödrön

Practices to Deepen:
- [ ] Loving-kindness meditation
- [ ] Body scan practice
- [ ] Journaling variations
- [ ] Creative expression
- [ ] Movement practices

Professional Support:
Consider working with:
- [ ] Therapist specializing in: _____
- [ ] Support group for: _____
- [ ] Coach focusing on: _____

Online Resources:
- [ ] Meditation apps: _____
- [ ] Online communities: _____
- [ ] Courses/workshops: _____

Online Resources:
- Crisis Line: 988
- Crisis Text: HOME to 741741
- Your therapist: _____
- Your support person: _____

Ways to Share Your Journey:
- [ ] Mentor someone beginning their journey
- [ ] Share your story (with boundaries)
- [ ] Create art from your experience
- [ ] Write about your transformation

A Letter From This Journal to You

Dear Brave Soul,

You've completed something remarkable. For 90 days, you've shown up for yourself in ways you may never have before. You've faced difficult truths, challenged old patterns, and chosen growth over comfort again and again.

This completion is not an ending but a commencement. You're graduating from guided practice to self-directed growth. You now have:

- **Tools that work** - tested through daily practice
- **Wisdom earned** - through experience, not just knowledge
- **Compassion cultivated** - through consistent self-kindness
- **Resilience built** - through navigating challenges
- **Joy reclaimed** - through intentional celebration

Remember:

- Progress isn't always linear
- Setbacks are opportunities for compassion
- You can always return to these pages
- The practices are yours forever
- You are worthy of the love you give yourself

The path continues, but you're no longer walking it unprepared. You carry within you everything you need. Trust the wisdom you've gained. Trust the tools you've mastered. Most importantly, trust yourself.

Some days will be harder than others. On those days, remember:

- You've done hard things before
- You have tools for every situation
- Support is available
- This too shall pass
- You are enough, always

Your journey of self-love is lifelong, not because you're broken and need fixing, but because you're human and deserve tending. Like a garden, you'll continue to grow, bloom, and transform with each season.

Thank you for trusting this process, for showing up even when it was difficult, and for choosing yourself again and again.

The world needs the authentic, self-loving version of you. Go forth and shine.

With deep respect and celebration,
You Are Enough: The 90-Day Self-Love Breakthrough

P.S. Remember—you can always begin again. Each day is Day 1 if you choose it to be.

What's Next?
- [ ] Rest and integrate for a week
- [ ] Review your toolkit and refine
- [ ] Set your 6-month practice plan
- [ ] Share your success with someone you trust
- [ ] Celebrate this incredible achievement

You've graduated from structured practice to self-directed growth.
Trust yourself. You're ready.

Congratulations on Your 90-Day Transformation

The beginning of your lifelong journey starts now...

Continue Your Self-Love Journey

You've completed 90 days of transformation. Why stop now?

Your journey doesn't end here. We've created additional journals, guided programs, and self-care tools to support your continued growth.

Explore our complete collection of wellness resources:

http://shop.thedailywellness.com

Find your next journal, gift one to someone you love, or discover new tools for your wellness practice.

Because you deserve support at every stage of your journey.

Special Thanks

Cover Design & Illustrations
Kaye Sanchez

Your artistic vision brought beauty and warmth to these pages, making the journey feel like coming home.

From Our Hearts to Yours

Thank you for trusting us with your 90-day journey. You've proven that self-love isn't just possible – it's your birthright.

Keep growing. Keep loving yourself. Keep being enough.

With gratitude and love,
The Daily Wellness Team

Ready for what's next?
http://shop.thedailywellness.com